THE GREAT BIOGRAPHERS

The
Great Biographers

By

ALBERT BRITT

Essay Index Reprint Series

BOOKS FOR LIBRARIES PRESS
FREEPORT, NEW YORK

First Published 1936
Reprinted 1969

STANDARD BOOK NUMBER:
8369-1077-X

LIBRARY OF CONGRESS CATALOG CARD NUMBER:
71-84300

PRINTED IN THE UNITED STATES OF AMERICA

To PRISCILLA

INTRODUCTION

BIOGRAPHY has become a popular subject. It has always been an interesting one. From the time of Plutarch down men have looked at other men and then tried to describe them. The beginnings naturally were crude. Material was scanty and the early efforts were full of guesses, hopes, and opinions which often led to sweeping conclusions. Saints and martyrs, of course, were usually the objects of biographical effort and the writer was committed in advance to a process of deification that has not yet disappeared. But, as readers have become more sophisticated, writers have become more cautious.

The realistic biography of today seems a far cry from Einhard's "Charlemagne" or Bonaventura's "St. Francis of Assisi." Nevertheless every biographer has sought with varying skill and honesty to present in his pages not only a man, but, so far as his vision and circumstances permitted, something of life itself.

Is biography literature or history? There is no satisfactory and complete answer. Perhaps it is both. The present book grew out of a course in biography at Knox College inspired by the chairman of the English department, who labored under the mistaken notion that the present writer knew something about biography. The making of the book began almost unconsciously, growing out of the necessity for crystallizing my own opinions about certain men, periods, and movements. The necessity of connecting one man and one period with another imposed itself and after two or three years a book began rather surprisingly to take form. It is not a textbook and it is not intended to be a complete guide to the study of biography. Perhaps it can best be described as a way of looking at biographies and biographers and a hint at the manner in which it is possible to find biographical reading interesting and at the same time a little informative.

I acknowledge my debt first to the students whose interest has given me courage to write. I am indebted, too, to the publishers from whose books I have quoted, particularly to William Morrow & Company, Inc., for permission to quote from Rupert Hughes's "Life of Washington,"; to Houghton Mifflin Company for the quotations from "The Quick and the Dead," "Wives," and "Damaged Souls," by Gamaliel Bradford, and "The Education of Henry Adams" by Henry Adams; to Harcourt, Brace & Company, Inc., for permission to quote from "Queen Victoria," "Eminent Victorians," and "Elizabeth and Essex" by Lytton Strachey; to Liveright Publishing Company for the quotation from "Henry VIII" by Francis Hackett; to D. Appleton-Century Company, Inc., for quotations from "Disraeli" by André Maurois; to G. P. Putnam's Sons for quotations from "Palmerston" and "The Second Empire" by Philip Guedalla.

ALBERT BRITT.

KNOX COLLEGE,
GALESBURG, ILL.,
December, 1935

CONTENTS

THE GREAT BIOGRAPHERS

I

WHAT IS BIOGRAPHY?

BIOGRAPHY as a subject of instruction is comparatively new. As an object of interest and of study, it has existed from the days of Plutarch and before. Probably the art of biography, in a crude sense, is as old as memory, coeval with articulate speech. Nothing could be more likely than that the old men of the tribe rehearsed the deeds of their heroic ancestors or of their own mighty youth around the campfire in the prehistoric caves of France and England. So far as the record runs, certain of the Old Testament writers, the writers of the synoptic Gospels, Xenophon in his "Memorabilia of Socrates," Plato in his account of the death of Socrates, Plutarch's "Lives," and Tacitus, in fragmentary fashion, are the known pioneers.

However, it is hardly fair to include all writing about men under the general heading of biography. If that were so, the "Odyssey" would rank high, as would the "Aeneid." In fact, one of the difficulties in this, as in the study of so many other arts, is to define objectives and to set a limit to the field of activity.

The word "biography" itself is comparatively new. The first record of its use is by John Dryden in his introduction to his translation of Plutarch, where he defines it as "the history of particular men's lives." The Oxford Dictionary adds little to this except a further limitation, "the history of the lives of individual men as a branch of literature." To identify biography with literature really adds nothing, at least until we have agreed more generally and more clearly as to what constitutes literature. At present we have gone little further than the rather vague belief that literature is somehow associated with the written word that by some miracle acquires vitality and influence, becomes touched with magic, as it were.

Carlyle, who practiced the art of biography assiduously, but frequently paid little attention to its limitations of time or space, characterized its place in these words: "The history of mankind is the history of its great men; to find out these, clean the dirt from them, and place them on their proper pedestal." It is possible to quarrel with the Scotch philosopher-historian's statement that part of the service of biography is to clean the dirt from the great men of history. To clean perhaps is reasonable enough, but not if the cleaning process is followed by a coat of whitewash.

And yet amid our difficulties of definition and limitation, that of marking the line where biography ends and advocacy begins is by no means the least difficult. In spite of his philosophical training and his apparent pre-occupation with problems of philosophy and theology combined, the redoubtable Carlyle was always a searcher for heroes and in his own twisted way a worshiper of them once they were found. For all his apparent burning desire for the betterment of common humanity, it was the great men that filled his vision. Somewhere he wrote: "Biography is the only history. Political history as now written and hitherto, with its kings and changes of tax-gatherers is little (very little) more than a mockery of our want."

The leap from Thomas Carlyle to André Maurois in search of a definition is not so rash as it might seem at first glance. To Carlyle life was at bottom a conflict of spirits, good and evil, in which the evil was constantly on the verge of victory. To the Frenchman it is a conflict of the spirit in which he is little concerned to discriminate between good and bad.

In both men the conflict is the absorbing, compelling thing. The chief difference seems to lie in their own reactions. Here they are then, Carlyle, brooding, morose, dyspeptic, at times despairing; Maurois, thrilled, exultant, enthusiastic, the perfect modern, comfortable in his orchestra chair in the third row from the front on the aisle. It is not surprising, therefore, to discover a kinship in their definitions of biography. To Maurois, "biography is a story of the evolution of the human soul; history should be for him [the writer] what it is for the portrait painter, the background against which he sets his model."

In all these definitions, as in all discussions of this particular art, there is one common thread, one principle on which there is universal agreement. In this case it is so obvious that it scarcely seems to require stating and perhaps so obvious that it is frequently ignored. The fundamental purpose of biography is to perpetuate the memory of a life. Surely nothing could be simpler than this, to take pen and paper and notes, letters, diaries, other materials, and with time and study to re-create a life so that it breathes and moves again on the printed page. And yet nothing is more difficult.

There are examples enough of the difficulties attending this process. Let us enumerate only a few. It is obvious at the outset that biography deals with the facts of a man's life. If he is not too long dead or was not by some curious trick of fate obscured by the cloud of his own achievements, as was Shakespeare, it should not be too difficult to discover the basic facts of a man's life. Nor is it, as a rule. In fact, biographers are more often swamped by an overabundance of material than starved by a lack of it. It is necessary also to make some kind of an appraisal of the value of particular material at a particular time. Few of us would care to have the story of our lives pitched in the key of our most immature years or our worst days or our more idle and mildly vicious moments. And yet there is a danger in such a general appraisal. It is so that myths are created. Through such a process of appraisal and reappraisal conducted in the praiseworthy spirit of high adoration, the mist-enwrapped figures of Washington and Lincoln rose up among us to a height from which it is impossible to bring them down so that we may again see them as they were to the men of their time.

Of course, one must have some picture of a man, a general mental portrait, if you please. In fact, it is seeing such a portrait in the mind that leads one first to select a subject for biography. When we say that a particular man interests us, we have confessed to such a process of appraisal. Such a preconception is harmless enough if it does not lead to the dangerous attempt to justify at the end the general picture with which the biographer began. This warning is hardly necessary for most of the biographers of today. Perhaps if it were written in reverse, it might be of more service.

Whether the verdict be flattering or otherwise, there is no doubt but that such a general pattern tends greatly to interfere with accuracy on the part of both writer and reader. As we look back at our own lives, we frequently see order and logic along the road of our experience, or in the experience of others, which is often the result of chance. Seen in perspective, events assume a relationship which they did not originally possess, and a writer demanding a logical scheme for his biography must beware lest he ascribe to the life which he describes a logic and an order which it possessed only as these were forced upon it from time to time by external events.

There are a few principles which perhaps can be set down as fundamental. First of all, biography must deal with what may be called the profane things of life. This is true even though one deals with religious figures or with men essentially occupied with matters of the spirit, as St. Francis, Ignatius Loyola, St. Augustine, St. Cuthbert, Joan of Arc, any or all of the saints of the calendar. The moment the biographer permits the moral earnestness or the theological convictions of his subject to enter too much into his own mind, his style becomes cramped and his accuracy subject to question. A biographer must, above all things, be interested in the affairs of this world rather than those of the next. He must seek vivid and arresting truths of portraiture rather than to express a sweeping estimate of the pure moral worth of his subject, however much he may happen to be impressed by the latter.

As Harold Nicolson, in his lectures on biography at Cambridge University, declares, biography must be intellectual and not emotional. "The moment that any emotion (such as reverence, affection, ethical desires, religious beliefs) intrudes upon the composition of a biography, that biography is doomed." To put the matter in another way, a biographer should not be concerned with moral judgments or conclusions any more than he may safely indulge in prophecy. If moral judgments and conclusions are to be derived fairly from an authentic presentation, the cause should be that of the subject and not the biographer.

An ever-present difficulty in the writing of biography lies in the obvious fact that the writer is quite as much of a complex personality, swayed by prejudices and hatreds and advocacies, as is his subject. Frequently the writing begins, as has been intimated, because of attraction or repulsion resulting from kinship or antagonism between writer and subject. Is it to be imagined for a moment that André Maurois wrote of Shelley and Disraeli and Byron merely because they were great Englishmen of the nineteenth century? And yet, with all apology to Maurois, there is a real danger in the attraction that drew him to these flamboyant figures.

And there is a third problem, that of the reader. Even if a book has only one reader, the equation becomes immediately complex. For one thing, it is evident to any publisher or writer of books that nothing is more difficult and probably undesirable than to compel a book to say to all its readers only that which the writer meant that it should say. And yet the moment this conflicting and entangling factor enters in, the possibilities of trouble multiply. Most writers desire with greater earnestness than is sometimes believed to tell the truth. If the books that were deliberately written for the purpose of misrepresenting the truth were heaped in one pile and burned, the resulting conflagration would offer much less illumination than is commonly supposed.

We are fond of referring to objective facts, but facts seldom remain objective for long unless it is their sad fate to be so uninteresting and unimportant that no one really takes them in and offers them a good home. An important fact soon becomes a personal possession, something to cherish, to die for, or perhaps something to be burned on the scaffold by the public hangman. This is peculiarly true in the case of biography. Edgar Lee Masters has been pilloried for his "Life of Lincoln," and yet the opinions he expressed were those held by many contemporaries of Lincoln and his statements of fact are substantially identical with those first printed by William Herndon, the loyal and admiring partner of Lincoln, and in large part repeated with documentary evidence by Mr. Albert J. Beveridge. Masters insisted on pointing a moral, whereas Herndon and Beveridge largely left it to their readers. Most students of Lincoln have already made up their minds before they read the first line of the first page.

Telling the truth is difficult because truth is not a simple thing. Certainly the truth of a man's life is not. It is made up of many days, strung together in groups of months and years. It is compounded from many single acts illustrated by letters, articles, newspaper interviews, state papers, poems, pictures, notes, incriminating letters to charming young ladies, all the rubbish of a man's life. And it is in this back yard of experience, heaped with good and bad, that the biographer must find the material with which to build his palace of beauty, if in fact it is such a palace that he is building.

Every fact in a man's life has a relationship to some other fact. Which fact is more important? And why? Lincoln, born in a log cabin, interested Europe after Europeans had come to a realization that this man was no mere backwoodsman, half horse and half alligator, nor a tree-dwelling ape; which is to say, after his death. And because he was born in a log cabin the chorus of wonder grew and the mists of awe and adoration clustered more thickly about him. As a matter of fact, the log cabin and even the rails which he split were useful adjuncts to the campaign of 1860, which resulted in Mr. Lincoln's becoming the wartime president of the United States. And they are of little more importance than that in a genuine understanding of Lincoln.

If one had sought matter for wonder in that primitive day in Illinois, he would more likely have found it had Lincoln lived in a brick house and not in a log cabin, for it was a log-cabin age and outside the few towns it was in log cabins that most of the population of Illinois lived. If the presidential candidate were to be chosen from Illinois at all, it is long odds that log cabins and rails and probably hard cider or whisky would have been found in close association with the experiences of his youth.

Telling the truth is no simple matter, particularly when it is the truth of color, relationship, ideal, or motive. And yet unless out of a biography the reader may select something that resembles such truths, it is safe to conclude that such a biography is for that reader an empty and a wooden thing. Parenthetically, we are here concerned primarily with the field of English biography, not because that is necessarily superior, although in my judgment no other nation has touched the high point reached in some of the great English lives, but chiefly for the reason that my primary interest is in biography as an expression of a people's genius, whether that be regarded as literary, historical, aesthetic, or a blend of all.

Of course, it is futile to attempt to draw too precise boundary lines. I have referred to André Maurois, whose lives of Shelley and of Disraeli have received and have merited so much attention. Bernard Faÿ's "Franklin, the Apostle of Modern Times" is certainly the latest, perhaps the last, word on the philosopher of the Revolution. Gilbert Chinard's "Thomas Jefferson, the Apostle of Americanism" is an illuminating work, more so perhaps because it has crossed the boundary of race and of language.

But in the main, the stream of English biography flows within fairly well defined banks. The springs from which it draws are likewise definite and on the whole easily located.

Of course, there is one name above all others in this list, that of Plutarch. It would not be easy to overestimate the significance of Plutarch and his "Lives" in this field.

II

THE PIONEERS

As I have said previously, biography is old. If
one cared to cite earlier examples, the story
of Joseph and his brethren in the Old Testament, the story of Samson, the Gospels, particularly the synoptic gospels, Matthew, Mark,
and Luke, might be cited. In a sense, the
narrative of the long wandering of the Israel-
ites in the wilderness is a biography of Moses.
In its qualities of realism, directness, and
definiteness of detail there is something almost
modern here. Of course, it is not possible to
ignore Xenophon's " Memorabilia of Socrates,"
and Plato's account of the death of Socrates
in the " Phaedo " is one of the classics.

It is to be doubted, however, if English
biography derives directly from these sources.
If any or all these had never existed or had
been lost to knowledge within the year that
saw them first committed to parchment, there
is still a strong enough current flowing out of
Plutarch to set in motion the full tide of life-

writing on which we float today. The significant contribution of Plutarch was not so much in the manner in which he did his work. To tell the truth, much of his writing is highly imaginative and at times slipshod and of course inaccurate. His original plan of selecting his men in pairs, one Greek, one Roman, and illustrating all the qualities of human genius and achievement thereby, is much too inelastic and tends too much to a dullness of repetition to deserve imitation. Fortunately Plutarch himself was too much on fire with the genuine merit of his idea to tolerate even so much of a scheme as he himself had provided. The result is that what the English-speaking world drew from Plutarch, even before the translations became available, was the conception of the lives of human beings as compelling, interesting, and in the main representative documents, reflections of life, and, so far as the reflections moved, life itself.

It was long after Plutarch that his work began to bear some fruit in England. In the meantime, what there was of biography in the early chronicles was from the artistic standpoint a poor thing of little worth. Most of it could be easily disposed of under the single term of hagiography, or literature of adoration. The people dealt with were practically without exception churchmen and the writers were also clerics.

There is a sufficient reason for this. In the dark days of the late Middle Ages in England and throughout the continent, only churchmen could write and, with a few exceptions, like Alfred the Great and Charlemagne, it was only churchmen who seemed worth writing about. Of course, the church was the custodian and protector of all literature, of all learning, of all art, of all that deserved permanence in a shifting and turbulent world.

However reasonable the phenomenon of hagiography, the results were anything but interesting from the standpoint of the modern student of general literature. An example is Adamnan's "Life of St. Columba." Columba was the first abbot of Iona Island, off the west coast of Scotland. Traditionally he was the first Christian missionary to the rough savages of the highlands. After his death, one of the earliest universities in Great Britain grew up around the abbey which he is alleged to have founded. Not many years ago an attempt was made to raise funds to re-create the University of Iona. The effort came to nothing and St. Columba remains the shadowy figure portrayed by Adamnan. Unfortunately, although almost a contemporary of Columba, Adamnan was little concerned with records, documents, matters of fact. When material failed he moralized; when it appeared necessary to impress his reader, he produced a miracle which, of course, was ascribed to the good saint.

There is an abundance of similar chronicles to be found buried, most of them, in the Latin of the time, containing little to reward anyone except the student concerned with intensive research and important to us only as part of the early trickle of the stream. There is the "Life of St. Patrick" by Muirchu Maccu Machthéni; the "Life of Wilfred, Bishop of York" by Eddius Stephanus; the "Life of St. Cuthbert" from Bede's "Ecclesiastical History"; the "Life of St. Guthlac" by Felix, and the so-called "Lives of St. Dunstan" by an unknown author or authors.

Then, of course, there is "Hugh of Lincoln," the greatest of hagiographies. This is the "Magna Vita" by Adam, Abbot of Eynsham. A little of the tinsel had worn off the hagiographic art by the thirteenth century when this was written and, although the good Adam deals largely in panegyric, he is nevertheless aware of the fact that Hugh of Lincoln was first a man and secondly a churchman and a statesman.

As has been said, there were two outstanding exceptions to the long line of churchmen as subjects for biography during this period. These were Alfred the Great and Charlemagne. Asser's "Life of Alfred" is no less a eulogy than many of the lives of the saints, but the secular character of Alfred's achievements gives a realistic note to the writing that is calculated to appeal to the more earthly mind.

An example of the attitude of such a writer as Asser, however, is given in his genealogy of Alfred. Not content with any mere Saxon pirate king or sea rover for his starting point, Asser begins with Adam and traces the descent generation by generation. This was not so difficult a task around the year 900, when every good Christian knew to a year the exact date of the creation of the world. Students who wish a thoroughly adequate version of Asser in English will find it in Edward Conybeare's "The Anglo-Saxon Chroniclers." The same volume contains extracts from the chronicles relating to Alfred.

Charlemagne, in his turn, was dealt with fully as gently as he deserved, although doubt-

less with no more glorification than his exploits
justified. His biographer was one Einhard,
frequently referred to as Eginhard, although
apparently incorrectly. Einhard, the author
of a document well known among students
of medieval Latin, "Vita Karoli," was a
student in the Palace School of Charlemagne
from 791 until the death of Charlemagne in
814 and probably for some time after under
Louis the Pious, Charlemagne's successor.
He extolls the virtues of the great emperor
in a manner that was quite to be expected
from a protégé and a dependent and is properly
myopic toward certain imperial shortcomings.
Some of his nearsightedness was due, of course,
to the age in which he lived. With the passing
of the centuries vices and virtues change faces
and places in a manner quite confusing to the
simple-minded reader who seeks not only a
single but a stable standard of morals. Einhard
is quite vague as to the name of one of the
imperial wives who was divorced and in
another passage admits that he has not yet
mastered the names of all the palace concu-
bines. His geography also is marked by the
vagueness of the time, but there is no uncer-
tainty in the passages in which he extolls the
mundane virtues and the spiritual achieve-

ments and consequent hopes of his great patron. His style is modeled admittedly on that of Suetonius and possesses the smoothness and careful phraseology of his model. Einhard is at least entitled to a place as a contemporary painter of a great man and on the whole a faithful chronicler of those aspects which he saw at close range, so far as he was able to understand them.

It is not well, however, for students of English biography to be unduly confident or critical in their attitude toward these early beginnings. With very few exceptions, it is only within our own century that the spell of hagiography has been entirely dissipated. There is reason to believe that it has not yet disappeared from the minds of many readers. The stream of criticism and abuse that broke over the head of James Anthony Froude when his ill-starred "Life of Carlyle" appeared can be attributed to nothing except whole-hearted adherence to the old belief in the undesirability of saying anything but good of the dead. Much of the objection to Paxton Hibben's "Henry Ward Beecher" centers not on questions of fact but on what the readers prefer to call good taste. Unpleasant statements should not be made about a dead man,

especially about a great preacher, even though
they are supported ten times over by the
record of fact. What is this but hagiology on
the part of the reader?

Sir Sidney Lee's "Shakespeare" is perhaps
the latest, it is to be hoped the last, outstanding example of hagiography. He permits no
question of the authenticity of every line
ascribed to Shakespeare, and the thought that
possibly some or many of the plays now bear-
ing the sacred name owed nothing to Shakespeare's authorship is a form of heresy. It
should be added in justice, however, to this
school of biography that the asset side of their
account is far in excess of the liability, considering the opportunities for error due to the
blindness of adoration. The world owes much
to the school of biography which presumably
came to an end at the beginning of the present
century.

It is natural, of course, that the early
biographical writings by and about church
fathers should be colored not only by the
theological concepts of the time but also by
the power and pervasive influence of ecclesiastical organization. An example is the "Life
of St. Francis of Assisi" written, or, more

properly, compiled, by St. Bonaventura in the latter part of the thirteenth century. By this time the Franciscan order had become powerful, not only through the general belief in the saintly character and effect of the life of its founder, but by virtue of the power of the order in a temporal or administrative sense.

About 1260 the Chapter-General of Narbonne, the central authoritative organization, decided that it was advisable to bring together the material of several fragmentary lives of the great mystic which had appeared during the latter part of his life and immediately after his death. This step appears to have been taken largely for a rather practical consideration. These fragmentary lives were contradictory as to fact, inconsistent as to spirit, and quite unsatisfactory in scope. The result of St. Bonaventura's work is a typical example of the quick growth of medieval tradition. There are abundant records of visions, as for example, of the leper by the roadside whom St. Francis embraced as a symbol of his love of the suffering and the poverty stricken. St. Bonaventura reports that after the embrace the leper promptly disappeared from sight. The implications of this episode are vague to the modern mind.

At another time a mysterious voice ordered St. Francis not to rest until he had repaired the church of St. Damian. This he did. Many instances are related of healing by touch, a common enough phenomenon in the Middle Ages when such powers were ascribed not only to the devout but to kings and princes whose devoutness was frequently subject to question.

The account of the founding of the order is characteristic of the time and of the chronicles of the time. According to St. Bonaventura's record, St. Francis opened the Gospels three times at random, noting each time the verse his eyes first rested on. These are the verses:

"If thou wilt be perfect, go and sell that thou hast, and give to the poor."

"Take nothing for your journey."

"If any man will come after me, let him deny himself, and take up his cross, and follow me."

There is here certainly sufficient reason for the vows of poverty which St. Francis took and which he imposed upon his followers. The incident of the opening of the Scriptures is highly credible. Throughout the Christian era men have sought guidance in this way in small things as well as large. More than one parent in colonial times and later found a name

for the new-born infant by opening the Holy
Writ at random and adopting the first name
that struck the eye. By no other method probably could such curious choices have been made.

The spirit in which the saintly biographer
took his work is fully and effectively stated in
this sentence from his Prologue: "For Francis,
even as the morning star in the midst of a
cloud, shining with the bright beams of his life
and teaching, by his dazzling radiance led
into the light them that sat in darkness and in
the shadow of death, and, like unto the rain-
bow giving light in the bright clouds, set forth
in himself the seal of the Lord's covenant."

In a spiritual and mystical sense, as well as a
literary, the "Confessions of St. Augustine"
deserve to rank with the "Life of St. Francis."
Chronologically, of course, they antedate it.
The spiritual message, except for the most
devout and spiritual of today, has long since
lost its meaning and remains, if it remains at
all, only as an interesting and authentic example of religious psychology. It is doubtful if
even the most earnest of modern preachers
could find here anything of value for his pulpit
use. Nevertheless the "Confessions" remain as
the seed of modern autobiography and this

seed contains in essence all of the qualities, including an overappreciation of the importance of the subject.

The arrangement of the book is roughly chronological, although the chronology is often obscured by the jumble of events, experiences, beliefs, visions, moralizing and, of course, the inevitable miracles. Between the lines are occasional vivid flashes that suggest the disordered, frequently violent, life of the earlier Middle Ages. St. Augustine has no doubts of his visions and his mission. Celestial voices spoke to him and celestial hands guided him. When he prospers it is because of this heavenly oversight and where he fails it is because he trusted to his earthbound powers.

But in the light of his contribution to the religious and temporal history of his time, there is probably stronger justification for autobiography here than in many other cases, and on the whole a more effective presentation of the material. The chief difficulty that it offers to the student of today is the fact that St. Augustine was concerned exclusively with matters of which the modern generation knows nothing and about which it cares nothing. All of which is probably more a criticism of our generation than of St. Augustine.

III

THE DAWN OF THE RENAISSANCE

THE Renaissance, which ushered in modern times, is a fruitful period of study from almost every aspect. In a discussion as narrow as this, it is not possible or desirable to define or more than vaguely to understand this curious upheaval that we have called the Renaissance. There is one aspect of it, however, which we must consider, that in which it is commonly labeled the revival of learning. The term is only partially descriptive. The phrase might better be written "revival of curiosity," for the fundamental fact of the Renaissance was the discovery that there were interesting things to learn.

There are two writers of this period of more than ordinary interest in the study of biography. One, the lesser known, is Giorgio Vasari. Vasari was born in Arezzo, Italy, in 1511 and died in 1574, a long life as lives went in that unhealthy day. Vasari was an artist, a protégé of the Medici and a pupil of Michel-

angelo and of Andrea del Sarto. After the
expulsion of the Medici from Florence, Vasari
was thrown upon his own resources and fell
easily into the vagabond current of the time,
wandering about Italy, painting portraits for
chance patrons, living generally the irresponsible, uncertain life of a talented gentleman of
the road.

The reconciliation of the Medici with Charles
V brought him back into favor and into regularity of living again and until Alessandro de
Medici was assassinated Vasari lived well as
the court painter of Florence. With the passing
of Alessandro there followed another period of
wandering succeeded by a somewhat uncertain
service of Pope Julius III and then again the
Medici, this time Cosimo, for whom he was the
architectural adviser. In this capacity he re-
modeled the Palazzo Vecchio and built the
Uffizi and on the death of Michelangelo became chief architect to St. Peter's in Rome.

It was during his second wandering, before
the return of Duke Cosimo de Medici, that
he appears to have conceived his plan of "The
Lives of Painters, Sculptors, and Architects"
and filled in the intervals of his vagabondage
with the gathering of material. Vasari has left
an autobiography in which he says that his

lives grew out of a conversation at the table of Cardinal Farnese at Naples in 1544. The work was completed in 1547. The lives number one hundred sixty-one in all, ranging from a few hundred to a few thousand words each. They include all the chief artists of his time and before, such as Giotto, Pisano, Orcagna, Luca della Robbia, Lorenzo Ghiberti, Brunelleschi, Filippo Lippi, Verrocchio, Pietro Perugino, Leonardo da Vinci, Fra Bartolommeo, Raphael of Urbino, Buonarroti, Titian, as well as many lesser lights who linger today as names, if so much. Many of the "Lives" deal with two or more artists in combination. The work ends with a chapter on "Divers Italian Artists," one on "Divers Flemish Artists," and a final "Description of the Works of Giorgio Vasari."

The manner of assembling the material made for a considerable degree of inaccuracy. For the most part Vasari's information was picked up by casual contacts compounded of rumor, legend, the injudicious praise of friends and the unfair censure of enemies. Sometimes he lumped together the work of two or three different men of different years and credited it all to one man. This is particularly true of the lesser artists. On the work of great men there was naturally a higher degree of accuracy

and a greater care in ascribing authorship.
The faults as well as the virtues of Vasari
contribute to the forming of an interesting
and, on the whole, accurate picture of the
artistic turmoil of the early Renaissance.

The number of names that he presents is in
itself testimony to the artistic activity of these
years when no village was so small as to be
without its artist and few artists so unimportant locally as to be lacking in pupils. His
style is easy, sometimes discursive and a little
gossipy. There is his anecdote of the remark
of Giotto to the King of Naples, when the
king, sitting for his portrait in the heat of the
Neapolitan summer, remarked: "Giotto, if
I were you this hot day, I would leave off
painting for a while." To which fatuous
observation Giotto replied pertinently: "So
I should certainly, if I were you."

Another artist who speaks out from the
midst of the Renaissance is more familiar to
the modern student, perhaps because he is
more himself a modern. This is Benvenuto
Cellini, practically a contemporary of Vasari,
but vastly different in the record that he has
left in the "Memoirs of Benvenuto Cellini."
Cellini wrote of the subject which most

interested him in all the world, himself. But
in writing of himself he has written unavoid-
ably and truthfully of his time. Born in
Florence in the year 1500, the son of a musician
and trained as a musician and goldsmith,
he appeared in Rome as a boy of nineteen
and attracted the attention of the Pope. Pope
Clement VII was then on the threshold of
his war with the Bourbons for the temporal
control of Italy, and Cellini enlisted on the
side of the Pope. He fought through the long
and bitter war that followed, presumably
acquitting himself bravely, but of course not
nearly so bravely as his autobiography indicates. In one passage he lays claim to killing
both the Constable of Bourbon and the Prince
of Orange. He claims to have been a prisoner
in the castle of St. Angelo in 1537 on a charge
of stealing jewels from the papal crown. He
escaped and was recaptured and, with more
counts against him than fell to the lot of the
usual prisoner, was on his way to the scaffold
and nearly arrived. This period of the memoirs
is regarded by most critics as highly imaginative and correspondingly inaccurate.

After the papal-Bourbon flames died down,
and Cellini had begun to acquire some fame
as a goldsmith, he was brought to the attention

of Francis I. Accordingly he shook the dust of Italy from his feet and sought fresh fame and greater profit in France, where he spent five unhappy years. From 1545 to the end of his life in 1571, he remained in Italy working by turns as sculptor, as cameo cutter, as engraver and painter or draftsman. He leaves no question in the mind of the reader of his autobiography as to his own excellence. He speaks casually of his turning to a new art, such as cameo cutting, and comments in his cocky fashion on the ease with which he acquired a remarkable proficiency due, as he admits, to his own native ability and his supreme mastery of the principles of all art.

Commissioned to model a button in gold for Pope Clement, he records: "I came forward, and opening a little round box; whereupon one could have thought that a light from heaven had struck the Pope's eyes. He cried aloud: 'If you had been in my own body you could not have done it better.'"

It is not merely such matters as this that Cellini records but much detail of his swaggering, lustful, fighting, drinking life. A musketeer had killed his brother. Let Cellini tell his story of revenge.

"This musqueteer lived hard by a place called Torre Sanguigna, next door to a house occupied by a courtesan, whose name was Signora Antea, one of the richest and most admired, and who made the greatest figure of any of her profession in Rome. Just after sunset, about eight o'clock, as this musqueteer stood at his door with his sword in his hand, when he had done supper, I, with great address, came close to him with a long dagger, and gave him a violent backhanded stroke, which I had aimed at his neck. He instantly turned round, and the blow falling directly upon his left shoulder, broke the whole bone of it, upon which he dropped his sword, quite overcome by the pain, and took to his heels. I pursued, and in four steps came up with him, when, raising the dagger over his head, which he lowered down, I hit him exactly upon the nape of the neck. The weapon penetrated so deep, that though I made a great effort to recover it again, I found it impossible; for at this same instant there issued out of Antea's house four soldiers with their swords drawn, so that I was obliged to draw mine also in my own defense."

An innkeeper offended him, possibly for demanding the payment of a bill. Cellini gained admission to the bedrooms of the inn and cut the beds to pieces with his poniard.

He lies without hesitancy, if lying seems indicated as the best means to advance his own interests or save his skin. And probably because of that he presents through his auto-biography the clearest picture that remains to us of the turbulent, uncontrolled life that throbbed through the streets of Renaissance Italy. It was a life of splendor as well as of wretchedness and debauchery, a life of great idealism as well as of great degeneracy. It was a time that produced some of the greatest visions of beauty here and hereafter that the world has seen. Cellini was a child of his time and a factor in that time.

Of his work little remains except the sculpture "Perseus," with the head of Medusa, in the Uffizi gallery in Florence, and a statue of Christ in the chapel of the Pitti Palace in Florence. Much that he did was fleeting and unimportant, a gold button for the cloak of a Pope or a cardinal, shoe buckles for a Medici prince or a visiting German noble, dies for coins and medals. But his journal is an immortal picture of a bravo and a man of talent.

The time when Cellini lived and wrote was a time of turmoil not only in Italy but through all Europe. There were three strong men playing for high stakes, no less than the control of the European world. These three were Henry VIII, Charles V, and Francis I. Probably a fourth should be added, Cardinal Wolsey, since for a time it was Wolsey rather than Henry who threatened to dominate the European scene from across the channel. And it is Wolsey who has remained the more sumptuous and dazzling character. He was fortunate to have in his entourage a gentleman usher by the name of George Cavendish. A gentleman usher in Wolsey's retinue was a mixture of doorkeeper, secretary, and familiar. In that capacity it was Cavendish's fortune to see and to hear most of what went on about the great cardinal, not only in his moments of power and confidence but in the hours of despair and weakness, which multiplied toward the end of his life. When other comforters failed there was always the young man at the door.

Three or four years of this sort of experience were Cavendish's. Born in 1500 he came with Wolsey as a young man of twenty-six or seven to remain with him to the end of his life in

1530. Twenty-seven years later, out of his
memories of his great master, he wrote "The
Life and Death of Cardinal Wolsey." Publishing was not safe or simple in that stormy
Tudor time, particularly when the book
to be published dealt not too gently with
Henry VIII and the other Tudors, and it was
not until 1641, when old animosities had died
or had been succeeded by the new ones of the
Stuart-Cromwell struggle, that Cavendish's
book first saw publication.

Even then it seems to have been brought out
not as a tribute to Wolsey, but as a warning to
Archbishop Laud of the fate that awaited too
arrogant princes of the church. But there were
over a dozen manuscript copies in existence.
Probably Shakespeare passed one of them
through his busy hands. Cavendish has Wolsey
say to Kingston on the day he died: "If I had
served God as diligently as I have done the
King, he would not have given me over in my
grey hairs." And at the close of the third act of
"Henry VIII," the dying cardinal says to
Cromwell: "O, Cromwell, Cromwell! Had I
but serv'd my God with half the zeal I serv'd
my King, he would not in mine age have left
me naked to mine enemies." It is at least
obvious that someone had read Cavendish and

that that someone had told Shakespeare what Cavendish said.

It is, of course, a prejudiced book. The three or four years in the train of the cardinal were all that Cavendish knew of courts and courtly splendor. After the death of Wolsey he retired to his estate in the country where he lived simply and in the kind of obscurity that was doubtless most welcome to one who had lived too close to danger. Here, of course, is the reason for the manuscript remaining so long unpublished. From the time the cardinal died until Cavendish put pen to paper, England had passed through the fires of religious persecution. The embers were still glowing. In fact, not until the last Tudor had passed from the picture and new names, new faces, new fears had filled the frame was it safe to tell so much as Cavendish had written.

The last paragraph in the book is illuminative of the spirit and character not only of the book but also of the man about whom it is written: "Here is the end and fall of pride and arrogancy of such men, exalted by fortune to honors and high dignities; for I assure you, in his time of authority and glory, he was the haughtiest man in all his proceedings that then lived, having more respect to the worldly honor of his person than he had to his spiritual profession; wherein should be all meekness, humility and charity; the process whereof I leave to them that be learned and seen in divine laws."

If one knew of Cardinal Wolsey only what is told in that sentence, one would still have in one's mind a clear picture of the tragic figure which he presented on the Tudor stage.

It is, of course, difficult always to rate works of art. No one may safely claim for this picture or that statue first place in any field or category. However, when one considers the conditions under which this life was written, the opportunities that the writer had for knowledge of his subject, the moving splendor, arrogancy, to quote Cavendish, and final tragedy of the great man about whom it was written, there is a strong temptation to say of Cavendish's "Life of Wolsey" that here certainly is the first of English biographies, not so much in order of merit as in historical importance and in the native power of the writer which shows throughout.

Compared with it, William Roper's "Life of Sir Thomas More," which is contemporary, is unimportant. In arrangement Roper is incoherent and incomplete, his motives more immediately partisan than those of Cavendish, his relationship to his subject more prejudicial. As More's son-in-law and trusted secretary he was in an excellent position to present to the world a picture of the powerful chancellor and intellectual interpreter of the Reformation in England, as he essentially was. In fact, Roper seems never to have heard of the Reformation or of Erasmus, More's constant correspondent. Although he must have read "Utopia," he fails to mention it. Possibly his ardent religious faith closed the windows to such cross winds of heresy.

Roper was exclusively concerned to clear the memory of his father-in-law of certain minor stains and shadows with the result that the reader of today finds himself wandering through a maze of fine-spun rationalizing about matters long since forgotten, matters which in fact ceased to be of importance almost before the ink was dry on Roper's manuscript. In addition, he is vague and often inaccurate on points of fact. An example is his placing the date of his father-in-law's execution in 1537 instead of 1535.

IV

WALTON AND THE DIARISTS

IF IT were possible to include all the attempts at biography and autobiography that should have been successful but were not, an important place would be given to the "autobiography" of Lord Herbert of Cherbury. Lord Herbert was a member of one of the great Elizabethan families and a sharer and at times an important factor in the life that carried over from the reign of the great queen nearly to the end of the Stuart regime. Born in 1583, he died in 1648, four years after the completion of his autobiography. The autobiography remained in manuscript until 1764, when it was published by Horace Walpole.

Herbert, one of a family of students and writers, a brother of George Herbert, poet and divine, Walton's "Pattern of primitive piety," was thoroughly imbued with an interest in philosophy at Oxford and throughout his life as courtier, diplomat, and soldier continued his studies and also wrote at considerable length. His "De Veritate" was declared worthy of Francis Bacon and he was an associate of the leading spirits of the Elizabethan reign from the polished wits of the court to the stars of the theater and the tavern —Ben Jonson, Fletcher, Marlowe, Shakespeare. His experience, as well as the character of his interest and mind, seems almost to demand an autobiography which should illuminate the intellectual life of his time. What he wrote was in reality an egotistical, swaggering record of duels, love affairs, social successes, and personal prestige, matters of no importance. There is hardly a line to suggest even an elementary knowledge of philosophy. One brief quotation is enough:

"Richard, Earl of Dorset, to whom otherwise I was a stranger, one day invited me to Dorset House, where bringing me into his gallery, and showing me many pictures, he at last brought me to a frame covered with green taffeta, and asked me who I thought was there; and therewithal presently drawing the curtains showed me my own picture; whereupon demanding how his lordship came to have it, he answered, that he had heard so many brave things of me, that he got a copy of a picture which one Larkin a painter drew for me, the original whereof I intended before my departure to the Low Countries for Sir Thomas Lucy."

The comparison with Cellini is unavoidable and entirely to the discredit of Lord Herbert. Where Cellini for all his fighting, his boasting, and his shamelessness remains the artist and the chronicler of his time, debonair, incisive, and interesting, Herbert achieved nothing but the chronicles of a swaggering braggart apparently ashamed of his own real accomplishments in more serious fields.

For all the promising beginnings shown by Cavendish and by such men as Cellini, Vasari, and even by Roper, biography was slow in following the secular signposts along the way. The safe road of piety still beckoned. Probably the stormy clouds that beset secular life in England during the greater part of the first half of the seventeenth century made piety doubly attractive to those who found little hope or comfort in temporal affairs. At any rate, there still linger some monuments of hagiography planted during this time. There is Thomas Fuller's "Lives and Deaths of Modern Divines" published about 1651. The subtitle is sufficiently descriptive: "Digested into one volume for the benefit and satisfaction of those that desire to be acquainted with the paths of piety and virtue." Both the "Modern Divines" and Fuller's "History of the Worthies," published in 1662, are embarrassingly shy on dates and facts.

Something similar might be said about Isaak Walton's "Lives" published at about the same time. This collection consists of five sketches dealing with John Donne, 1640; Sir Henry Wotton, 1651; Richard Hooker, 1665; George Herbert, 1670; Robert Sanderson, 1678. The writing of these sketches was an old-age diversion of the author of "The Compleat Angler." In fact, he was eighty-five years old when the life of Sanderson was written.

Walton was born in 1593 in London and was a shopkeeper until the fifty-first year of his life. There is no evidence that his literary ambitions had any result until near the time of his retirement. The date of the sketch of Donne, 1640, places the author somewhere in his forty-seventh year and within four years of his retirement from business. He appears to have had ample opportunity to know many men in London but to have confined his acquaintance largely to ecclesi-

astics or to those concerned with theological
matters. His age would have permitted him
to have seen Shakespeare, but it is doubtful
if he ever heard of the Bard of Avon except
perhaps as a vagabond player whom it was
much better not to know.

Only one of the five men whom he selected,
Sir Henry Wotton, was not directly connected
with the church and even in this instance
Walton manages to make out a fair case for
the pietistic and humanistic qualities of the
traveler, diplomat, soldier, and poet. Wotton
was a follower of the Earl of Essex and was
with him in Ireland on the ill-fated expedition
with which he was to dazzle Elizabeth. When
Essex was arrested at the order of the queen,
Wotton fled to Italy where he remained in
exile until after the queen's death. Walton
makes singularly little of the events of Wotton's life abroad and suggests by implication that his exile was chiefly valuable as
affording opportunity for quiet contemplation.
A long and difficult trip made by Wotton from
Italy to Scotland as a messenger from the
Duke of Florence to the King of Scotland
to advise the latter of a plot against his life is
dealt with as casually and briefly as though it
were nothing but a summer afternoon's stroll.

After the beginning of the second Stuart regime and Wotton's return to England, he became Provost of Eton College. It is really this phase of his life that interests Walton, that demure lover of quiet streams and shady paths. Of this phase of Wotton's career Walton says: "A college was the fittest place to nourish holy thoughts and to afford rest both to his body and mind." This may have been true in the seventeenth century.

The other lives are similar in general character. Donne, Wotton, and Hooker were all three personally known to Walton and in the case of Donne particularly, the writer must have been familiar with some of the agonies of that queer, twisted, tortured soul that found expression in his verse. There is no indication, however, in Walton that Donne was anything more than another leisurely follower of quiet streams, another gentle wanderer on the bypaths of life.

Herbert, the poet preacher and brother of Lord Herbert of Cherbury, is characterized as "that pattern of primitive piety."

It is easy to dismiss Walton as does Mr. Nicolson as a writer of autobiography posing as biography or as Sir Walter Raleigh, lecturer at Oxford called him, "a writer of obituary poems." Raleigh was a difficult and caustic critic who found few things to please him and who refused to subsist on fractional satisfactions. And Nicolson is too much a modern to be willing to ascribe quite full credit to pioneers in his chosen field.

It needs to be said, therefore, that with all his faults, with all his intrusion of his own character, Walton was a pioneer. To be sure, he found too many reflections of his own naïve, quiet nature. He fits his subjects too much and too often into his own quiet, simple ethical mold. He had perhaps little insight into fact and little practical vision or sense of actuality. But for all that he was the first Englishman to write deliberate biography without the compulsion of some sense of loyalty or of kinship such as impelled Roper and Cavendish. And he is entitled to at least the kind of memorial tablet that we erect to pioneers. The fact that the tablet might be erected with some sense of relief that we are permitted to honor the pioneers rather than to live with them need not alter the sincerity of the memorial.

Of course, there is one outstanding figure in the seventeenth century gallery. The prince

of all diarists, gossips, if you please, auto-
biographers, and social historians, was one
Samuel Pepys. Pepys was the son of a London
tailor. He was born in 1633 and died in 1703.
He seems to have possessed the rare faculty
of being sufficiently able to give a good account
of himself throughout his life, to know the
right people, to do the right things, to be seen
in the right places at the right times but
seldom to his own disadvantage. Perhaps
his motto was that of Aristotle: "Nothing
too much."

The period in which he lived was one of
storm and change, from Stuart to Commonwealth, from Commonwealth to Stuart, and
from Stuart to Orange. Pepys weathered them
all, except for a brief term in the Tower in
1679 for alleged complicity in an alleged
popish plot. Apparently there was at least one
allegation too many. At any rate, Pepys was
soon at liberty.

His education was excellent—St. Paul's,
then Magdalen at Cambridge. Throughout
most of his life he was a government servant
important enough for his own profit after the
rather loose habit of the time and not so
important as to share the misfortunes of the
too great. The year 1647 saw him Clerk

of the Privy Seal under Cromwell; 1665 saw him Surveyor General under a Stuart; 1686 to 1688 saw him Secretary of Admiralty under another Stuart. The Revolution of 1688 ended his public service but brought him no greater disaster than was involved in abundant leisure for the quiet work of his old age. The chief fruit of this was his "Memoirs of the Navy" published in 1690.

Of course, the great contribution of Pepys, the sole reason for remembering him, is his immortal "Diary." This covers the period from January 1, 1660, to May 31, 1669. It was written in cipher and remained untranslated until 1825, when it was deciphered by John Smith and edited by Lord Braybrooke. It was not until 1893 that the "Diary" as now known was printed. There are unprintable fragments that still remain and will probably continue unprinted indefinitely. The original "Diary" is in the possession of Magdalen College at Cambridge, which owns also Pepys's library presented to the college after his death. The official title is ponderous but descriptive: "Diary of Samuel Pepys, F. R. S., Secretary to the Admiralty in the reign of Charles II and James II. The diary deciphered by the Rev. J. Smith, A. M. from the Original

Shorthand MS. in the Pepysian Library. With notes by Richard Lord Braybrooke."

The diary is a mixture of gossip, scandal, wire-pulling, licentiousness, and chronicles of serious matters seriously set down. Pepys lived through the Great Fire and the Great Plague and describes them both in his Diary. He saw King Charles beheaded at Whitehall in 1649 and in 1660 saw General Harrison beheaded at Charing Cross, "the first blood shed in revenge for the King." He was an insatiable theatergoer. He writes of first nights, the players on the stage, the nobility in the boxes. All the gossip of the court came to his ears. Much of it he records. His "Diary" depicts the swift decay of the English navy in the years immediately following the Stuart return.

His tastes and interests are catholic and his entries range from the most trivial to the most important. On October 13, 1660, he writes: "I went out to Charing Cross to see Major-General Harrison hanged, drawn, and quartered; which was done there, he looking as cheerful as any man could do in that condition. He was presently cut down, and his head and heart shown to the people, at which there was great shouts of joy. It is said, that he said that he was sure to come shortly at the right hand of Christ to judge them that now had judged him; and that his wife do expect his coming again. Thus it was my chance to see the King beheaded at Whitehall, and to see the first blood shed in revenge for the King at Charing Cross. Setting up shelves in my study."

On December 1 he favors us with a domestic episode: "This morning, observing some things to be laid up not as they should be by my girl, I took a broom and basted her till she cried extremely, which made me vexed; but, before I went out I left her appeased. Went to my Lord St. Albans's lodgings, and found him in bed, talking to a priest, (he looked like one) that leaned along over the side of the bed; and here I desired to know his mind about making the katch [ketch] stay longer, which I got ready for him the other day. He seems to be a fine, civil gentleman. There fell into our company old Mr. Flower and another gentleman, who did tell us how a Scotch Knight was killed basely the other day at the Fleece in Covent Garden, where there had been a great many formerly killed." The Fleece was a low tavern in Covent Garden which John Aubrey neatly describes as "very unfortunate for homicides."

So the entries run, frequently unrelated, serious, frivolous, grave, gay, comic, tragic, all the color and incident of the life of a busy gossip.

There was another diarist of Stuart and Cromwell England more thorough and detailed but not so great as Pepys. This was John Evelyn. Evelyn lived practically through the century, born in 1620 and dying in 1706. His diary began in 1641 and continued to within a few months of the end of his life. He was the son of a wealthy man, landowner, country magnate, and devoted adherent of the Stuarts. His education was of the conventional Oxford variety at Balliol and for a short time he was enrolled in the Middle Temple.

Although a devoted royalist throughout his life, he seems to have been disturbed little except in spirit by the civil wars and continued to live at his pleasure in England through the reign of the Lord Protector. His public service began in the reign of the Stuarts in 1660 and for several years following he was on many government commissions which were apparently not without profit for his labors as well as occupation for his leisure hours. He wrote one other work of considerable compass, a

"History of Navigation and Commerce," and also translated the "Mystery of Jesuitism" and had his name attached to a number of pamphlets and treatises on various subjects.

His diary is a detailed, frequently dull, exact entry day by day of what he did and where and when, whom he saw, frequently of what he ate and wore, and sometimes the direction of the wind and the state of the weather. There is little of the living, whimsical human interest that characterized Pepys and still less anything that was in any way libelous or otherwise likely to bring the writer into difficulty. Those portions of his diary that were written during his brief experience in the Dutch Wars with Spain and his travels in France and Italy read like a mixture of diary and guidebook. In fact, much of his description of churches, statuary, palaces, and monuments of various sorts in Italian cities could hardly have been secured except from some seventeenth century equivalent of Baedeker.

There are occasional mild personal touches which fitfully illuminate the rather wearisome task of the chronicler. At Oxford he saw the Greek Conopios, legate from the patriarch at Constantinople. There is nothing to indicate the mission of the legate or his character or

conduct, but there was one item about him
that impressed itself on Evelyn: "He was the
first I ever saw drink coffee, which custom
came not into England till thirty years after."
This entry is dated 1637. Gastronomic historians should note this as an important date
in their favorite subject.

Another figure of the Stuart return was the
Duke of Newcastle. The Duke appears to have
been a worthy gentleman of many accomplishments, particularly in the training of horses,
loyal to his king provided it were not too
much trouble, and above all jealously sensitive
of his own rights and prerogatives. He, like
many another, would long since have been
forgotten, dust blown on the wind of history,
if it were not for his good fortune in finding a
biographer. In fact he married her. Margaret,
Duchess of Newcastle, was the noble dame to
whom Charles Lamb referred as "that princely
woman, the thrice noble Margaret Newcastle."
Another phrase with which Lamb labels her is
apparently one that pleased him mightily,
"original-brained." It is almost as difficult for
us of today to understand the gentle Elia's
fondness for Margaret, Duchess of Newcastle,
as to be interested in Margaret herself. Her

book, "The Life of the First Duke of Newcastle," is a panegyric, jealous, sweeping in its
condemnation of enemies, unstinted in its
praise of the duke.

Newcastle was one of Charles I's generals
who was exiled during the Commonwealth
and returned with Charles II to spend the
closing years of his life in attempting to
recapture his estates. Margaret married the
duke in exile as his second wife, and devoted
herself to clearing his reputation. Both Pepys
and Evelyn refer to the stir caused by her
public appearances in London, her eccentric
dress, her brilliant but unstable conversation,
her unflinching refusal to be obscured no
matter what the cost of publicity. Pepys says
of her: "The whole story of this lady is a
romance and all she does is romantic. . . .
There is as much expectation of her coming to
Court, that so people may come to see her, as
if it were the Queen of Sheba."

Evelyn's comment is more caustic: "Her
mien surpasses the imagination of poets, or the
descriptions of a romance heroine's greatness;
her gracious bows, seasonable nods, courteous
stretching out of her hands, twinkling of her
eyes, and various gestures of approbation,
show what may be expected from her dis-

course, which is as airy, empty, whimsical
and rambling as her books, aiming at science,
difficulties, high notions, terminating commonly in nonsense, oaths, and obscenity."

A sample of her praise of the duke is:
" . . . in all actions and undertakings where
my Lord was in person himself, he was always
victorious and prospered in the execution of
his designs; but whatsoever was lost or succeeded ill, happened in his absence, and was
caused either by the treachery, or negligence
and carelessness of his officers." Granting
such an attitude, the task of the biographer is
simple.

The diarists are not entirely fair to the
eccentric duchess, although naturally her
eccentricity was quite as well calculated to
bring her criticism as popularity. Her writing
was not inferior to that of many other successful writers of the time and her courage
certainly beyond question. She wrote several
plays, at least one of which, "Love's Adventures," had dramatic merit. Her verse is hardly
worth recalling. Her references to the duke are
sometimes more vividly descriptive than the
noble lady could realize.

Here is a perfect picture of the titled
Englishman of the time: "His education was

according to his birth; for as he was born a gentleman, so he was bred like a gentleman. To school-learning he never shewed a great inclination; for though he was sent to the university, and was a student of St. John's College in Cambridge, and had his tutors to instruct him; yet they could not persuade him to read or study much, he taking more delight in sports than in learning."

Not even Pepys can surpass in simplicity and effectiveness the paragraph in which the duchess describes the return of the duke to England in the train of King Charles in 1660:

"At last being come so far that he was able to discern the smoak of London, which he had not seen in a long time, he merrily was pleased to desire one that was near him, to jogg and awake him out of his dream, for surely, said he, I have been sixteen years asleep and am not thoroughly awake yet. My Lord lay that night at Greenwich, where his supper seemed more savoury to him than any meat he had hitherto tasted; and the noise of some scraping fidlers, he thought the pleasantest harmony that ever he had heard."

V

ENTER THE EIGHTEENTH CENTURY

IT HAS become the fashion recently to discover the eighteenth century. Students of poetry, of the theater, of art, of politics, of religion, even of science are finding in the years that stretch from Queen Anne to George III the fruitful source of new hopes and the beginnings of new worlds. It was a century in which the English-speaking world awoke to many new possibilities, among others the possibility of revolution. England enjoyed through the first half of the century an unusual respite from foreign wars and domestic violence. The German kings were content to rule and live in England as little as possible. George I spoke no English. George II was little bette r Neither of these rotund, irascible gentlemen had any love for England or the English. English cooking, in particular, offended them and English beds were the last word of discomfort. As a consequence they were content to draw their civil list allowance, to open Parliament, to hold occasional levees, to ride in the royal coach in occasional processions through London streets. Beyond this they cared little. The government of England during most of this half century rested in the hands of one Robert Walpole, hard-fisted, hard-living, high-handed, proud, un-flinching, honest, highly patriotic Englishman.

Walpole was of the breed of three-bottle men. He said of himself that as a young man at his father's table he was required to drink two glasses of wine to his father's one because the elder Walpole held to the old-fashioned belief that no son should ever see his father drunk. There was one fixed principle in Walpole's mind and that was that England, the England that he loved more than most public men of his time, the England of the manor, the peaceful countryside, the sleepy villages, should have a chance to rest and renew her strength. There were to be no foreign wars. There were to be no offensive tax levies for army or navy. There were to be no flashy and expensive expeditions against the French of Canada or the Dutch of the East Indies or the Spanish of South America. That was to come later. Now England must rest and rally her strength, save her money, save her man-power.

It is a pity that there is no adequate biography of Robert Walpole. He deserves it more than most. If it had not been for this hard-headed, narrow-minded, faithful Englishman it is more than possible that England might have frittered away her strength in tuppeny wars about the world, leaving her little reserve when the day of judgment came at Quebec and Louisbourg and later at Trafalgar and Waterloo.

For our purposes it is enough probably to characterize the eighteenth century as a century of awakening. Printing was cheaper than ever before and reading more common. For the first time in a hundred years or more men had safe leisure. Much of it they spent in coffeehouses, in clubs, where talk ranged widely, stimulating curiosity and leading to further talk. It was natural that much of this gossipy conversation should find its way to paper. Some of these still survive under the title of Characters, short sketches, sometimes accurate accounts of living men, frequently half fiction.

It was in 1714 that Alexander Smith appeared with a "History of the Lives of the most noted Highwaymen, Footpads, Housebreakers, Shoplifters, etc." The title is tempting enough to justify Walter Raleigh's comment that "modern biography was established."

Edmund Curll achieved a considerable prominence as publisher and writer of brief scurrilous biographies, of which he wrote fifty or more. Curll was apparently a low sort of journalist who happened on the value of the material that lies in the lives of ordinary individuals. Most of his discoveries were criminals. This was the century when hangings were public festivals and hawkers sold badly printed pamphlets through the crowded streets telling in highly colored language of the lives, startling exploits, and sensational deaths of the headliners of Newgate or Ludgate. Walter Raleigh sums up Curll's career succinctly: "It occurred to him that, in a world governed by mortality, men might be handsomely entertained on one another's remains."

Defoe served his apprenticeship in this kind of unpromising, usually anonymous authorship, of which his lives of Jack Sheppard and Jonathan Wild are examples. It is probable that his experience in delving into the records of criminals and seeking out sordid facts with a vivid imagination first led his thoughts to

the possibilities of fiction. After all, the step
from Jack Sheppard to Moll Flanders is not
a long one. It was not only an easy step from
scurrilous biography to scurrilous fiction, but
with the idea of biography in the air it was
natural that more respectable permanent
work should be done.

There was Roger North, for example, with
his lives of his three brothers. "Francis, the
good judge; Sir Dudley, the merchant ad-
venturer; Dr. John, the weak and unfortunate." The terms of characterization are
North's own. It is natural that Dr. John,
"the weak and unfortunate," should be the
most interesting.

John Aubrey's "Miscellanies" published
a little earlier is in the form of scattered notes
and fragmentary entries written at odd times
at the request of Anthony Wood who was pre-
paring material for his "Athenae Oxonienses."
The character of the "Miscellanies" is sufficiently indicated by some of the subjects he
discussed: "Apparitions, Impulses, Knockings,
Blows Invisible, Prophecies, Marvels, Magic,
Transportation in the Air, Visions in a Bevil
or Glass, Converse with Angels and Spirits,
Corps-Candles in Wales, Glances of Love and
Envy, and Second-sighted Persons in Scot-

land." Nothing was ever finished for Aubrey was, as Wood said of him, "a shiftless person, roving and magotie-headed." It was not until 1898 that this biographical material was brought together and published in a collected form by Andrew Clark under the title of "Short Lives." Aubrey had one central thought, that biography should be contemporary, truthful, and interesting. However, his attention was too easily diverted, his intellectual processes too eccentric, his interest too unstable for him to contribute much more than vague beginnings and uneven performances.

Unimportant as Aubrey's sketches are, they moved Lytton Strachey to say in his brief sketch of the author in "Portraits in Miniature":

"The method of enormous and elaborate accretion which produced the Life of Johnson is excellent, no doubt; but, failing that, let us have no half-measures; let us have the pure essentials—a vivid image, on a page or two, without explanations, transitions, commentaries, or padding."

The eighteenth century saw the beginning of the biographical dictionary, the "Biographia Britannica," under the editorship at first of

William Oldys, the author of a "Life of Raleigh," a solid, thorough, and uninteresting piece of antiquarian work. Horace Walpole constructed his "Catalogue of Royal and Noble Authors" and Samuel Johnson published his "Lives of the Poets."

Cibber's chief place in the eighteenth century gallery is due to his autobiography, "An Apology for the Life of Colley Cibber." He was a product of London and his book deals largely with the theater of the first quarter of the century. He saw the institution grow from the plaything of kings and princes to something that promised to become self-respecting and self-sustaining. He knew it at the time when to be an actress was regarded as practically equivalent to a confession of loose living. It was at about the time of his birth in 1671 that it began to be possible for a woman of either good or bad character to appear on the stage. When he died the profession was established and there was no need to apologize.

Cibber knew the theater from the inside. Having failed of admission to New College at Oxford he began as an apprentice in a London theater, working nine months without pay.

He records his first salary as ten shillings a week. His first part was the chaplain in the "Orphan of Otway." He was by turns star, playwright, producer, critic. In all these capacities he was self-confident, self-sufficient, and on the whole capable. His standard for the theater was by comparison high and self-respecting. Pope libeled him in "The Dunciad." Johnson and Fielding sneered at him, Johnson declaring, "Taking from his conversation all that he ought not to have said, he was a poor creature," but Swift, the most powerful intellect of them all, sat up all night to read his "Apology." The book is uneven with long stretches of dullness and many paragraphs about quarrels and jealousies long since forgotten. But it is also rich with material on London and the theater of the time. Cibber was frank, foolish, fitful, vain, but in the main honest.

One of the minor literary milestones of the eighteenth century in respect to method, at least, was John Mason's "Life of Gray." Mason's contribution was in his use of letters as the basis and in large part the substance of his writing. Hitherto the chief effort of the crude biographer had been to express his opinion or conclusion. If material presented itself substantiating such opinion, it was received with gratitude. Otherwise the opinion was expressed without support. Contrary evidence in letters or documents was largely ignored.

Mason's plan was simple and also obvious to us in the present day. It was nothing more than permitting Gray, through his letters and the replies, to tell his own story. Unfortunately Mason lacked the courage of his own idea and his preconception of the poet, and, still more, his overweening estimate of the value of respectability and regularity on the part even of a poet prevented him from giving his original intention full enough scope. Embarrassing paragraphs were omitted, statements which failed to accord with his original outlines were omitted or altered, and in some cases phrases and passages were introduced tending, in Mr. Mason's view, to present more clearly the picture of the poet as he, Mason, thought he should be.

Excellent as it was for its time, Mason's book is primarily the work of a friend and advocate. But it did one unforgettable thing, it gave the key for a new method in biography, a method which, as Nicolson says, threw upon

the reader "the onus of drawing his own conclusions," and incidentally, gave him the
opportunity of reaching quite different conclusions from those of the writer, although
drawn from the same material. And he opened
the way for James Boswell.

Oliver Goldsmith did better than Mason.
His lives of Voltaire, Richard Nash, Thomas
Parnell (the poet), and Lord Bolingbroke,
though light in style and also slight in substance, were probably the best that had been
written since Walton and as documents of
human life far superior to the work of the
pious angler. But history retains its impression
of poor Noll as a brilliant blundering fool and
full justice is not likely to be done him as the
able, appreciative, creative thinker that he was.

VI

JOHNSON AND BOSWELL

IT REMAINED for one man to set the pace for
the new biography. That was Samuel Johnson.
In him the eighteenth century culminated
more than in any other man and without him
English literature of that period would have
lost not only color but substance and direction.
His "Lives of the Poets" are as much land-
marks in the field of biography as the plays of
Shakespeare in dramatic literature or Milton
in poetry. To appreciate this it is necessary
to attempt a contemporary point of view.
The fact that now no one except a student of
English literature reads what he has to say of
Pope or Savage or the rest does not alter the
importance of Johnson at the time of writing.
His "Lives" were all brief in compass but
packed with material. He wrote them as
introductions to editions of the poems and
designed them not only as summaries of the
biographical facts but as critical guides to the
poet's work and an aid to the reader who would
appreciate or compare.

As Lytton Strachey says of him, he brought to his work "immovable independence of thought—his searching sense of actuality." It was the last that was the genuinely new thing in the field of criticism. Previously criticism, like kissing, had gone by favor. To Johnson, poetry and literature in general were far too important to be tossed about on the waves of friendship or of envy. The sense of actuality to which Mr. Strachey refers might perhaps as well be called a sense of importance, for Johnson had little interest in the realities of detail and the fine distinctions of fact or relationship to be determined only by careful grubbing in dusty manuscripts. The crabbed philosopher was no research expert. Nevertheless his sense of importance carried with it a rare power of discernment of fraud, as well as of excellence.

His attitude toward the alleged poetry of Ossian is a case in point. At bottom, his denunciation of James Macpherson, who claimed to be the discoverer and translator of the work of the first Irish bard, rested on the sturdy belief that Macpherson's claims could not be true primarily because they were the sort of thing that could not be true, and that they had no merit even if they were true.

As a critic he was rather more original than as a philosopher. Experiments in poetic forms found little favor in his eyes, as did experiments in most other fields, for Johnson was a staunch supporter of the established order in art, religion, politics, and in society. His "Life of Alexander Pope" is probably as good an example of his method as any other. First there is the detailed description of the poet and his appearance as small, deformed, sensitive, bad-tempered, exacting, and prudent. Then follows a discussion of the poet's work with much emphasis on the method and style, giving scope to the poet's slow, careful choice of subject, his habit of careful revision, his care in the use of words, narrow range of style, and generally conventional philosophy, both social and literary. It was natural that Johnson should like Pope. He says of him: "Every other writer [except Dryden] since Milton must give place to Pope."

This passage is cited not so much as an appraisal of Pope as a reflection of Johnson's attitude and an indication of the literary and artistic poverty of the time. Johnson's style was fixed, conventional, and frequently epigrammatic. He denounces the idle or indecent use of scriptural allusions in a characteristic phrase: "A mode of merriment which a good man dreads for its profaneness and a witty man disdains for its laziness and vulgarity." He sums up his attitude toward the poet in another characteristic epigram: "Those who could not deny that he was excellent, would rejoice to find that he was not perfect."

There were in all fifty-two of these lives, all written with great speed and under high pressure, but all marked by the same dogged persistence of method and power of philosophical infiltration that always characterized Johnson. His literary output was extraordinarily large even in that time when men were intoxicated over their discovery of the ease of printing. He boasts of the production of his Dictionary singlehanded in less time than was usually occupied for similar work in other countries with a large staff.

His "Rasselas," "Rambler," and "Idler" were much read and even his poems, ponderous and awkward as they were, were not without praise. Much of his writing was purely ephemeral and failed to last out the year which saw it committed to print. It is one of the revenges of time that Johnson, the figure of the eighteenth century, the one man in whom the life of London coffeehouses, the streets, and the studies seemed to concentrate, should owe a large part of his immortality to a garrulous Scotchman, half barrister, half literary man, and altogether parasite, and yet after all a bit of a genius.

James Boswell was born in Ayrshire, in the county of Burns. He was educated in Edinburgh, the first heaven of all ambitious and restless Scotchmen, and passed the greater part of his life in London, the ultimate Scotch paradise. His knowledge of law was chiefly that of a student, as there is no record of his practice. His real passion in life was to talk with gifted men and women and as far as possible to eat and drink at their expense. With it all he was gay, convivial, witty, somewhat naïve, often foolish but never a fool, and always a prodigious writer-down of conversation, experience, and observation, and he was not to be rebuffed. No indignity was too great if, by enduring it, he could reach the side of the desired great man.

He met Johnson first in 1763 and in his record of the event compares the experience to the line in which Horatio warns Hamlet of the coming of his father's ghost: "Look, my lord, it comes." Johnson was characteristically abrupt and rude on this occasion and Boswell confides to his diary: "Had not my ardour been uncommonly strong, and my resolution uncommonly persevering, so rough a reception might have deterred me forever from making any further attempts."

All in all, Boswell was associated with Johnson, sometimes as close friend and confidant, over a period of twenty years from the first meeting in 1763. About two-thirds of Johnson's life was finished before Boswell set eyes on him, but out of the material of the other third Boswell fashioned immortality. Even our knowledge of the physical appearance of Johnson we owe in large part to Boswell: "His brown suit of cloaths looked very rusty; he had on a little old shriveled unpowdered wig, which was too small for his head; his shirt-neck and knees of his breeches were loose; his black worsted stockings ill drawn up; and he had a pair of unbuckled shoes by way of slippers."

Those who have declared the Boswellian life merely the product of a blind friend and sycophant will have trouble enough in explaining away this characterization. There are more such phrases displaying an acuteness on the part of Boswell that is not always

ascribed to him by his critics, as for example:
"Praise, in general, was pleasing to him; but
by praise from a man of rank and elegant
accomplishments he was peculiarly gratified."

An amusing interlude is Boswell's description of the clever way in which he arranged to
bring Johnson and John Wilkes, the pamphleteer, together. Johnson had been unsparing
in his denunciation of Wilkes and almost
equally so in his condemnation of those who
gave him either political or social countenance.
Mr. Dilly had arranged for a meeting of
Johnson and Wilkes at a dinner at his house
and it was Boswell's task to bring it about.
He paved the way first by inviting Johnson,
then by suggesting that he might like to know
who the other guests were to be, at which
Johnson flew into a rage and demanded to
know by what right one guest dared inquire
about the other guests or question the right
of his host to invite whom he chose. "What
do you mean, Sir? What do you take me for?
Do you think I am so ignorant of the world
as to imagine that I am to prescribe to a
gentleman what company he is to have at his
table?" Thus was Johnson's fire drawn in
advance of his meeting with the pamphleteer
at Mr. Dilly's table.

In this case Boswell's drama is complete, the prologue being the clever scheme by which he outwits the prejudice of Johnson; the body of the play is the dinner itself with the witty shrewd talk which gives the point and color of the occasion. If Boswell is not a master of English, he is at least an artist in presentation, which after all is the same thing—if not a better thing.

So goes the biography, page after page, shrewd, witty, ill-tempered sayings by Johnson, descriptions of the great man not always flattering, as we have seen, light touches at other great figures of the time, Edmund Burke, David Garrick, Edward Gibbon, Oliver Goldsmith, Joshua Reynolds, all of the figures that ate and drank about the tables of London coffeehouses. These names still remain. It is still possible to eat and to drink at the tables of one of their houses, the Cheshire Cheese, now devoted largely to the entertainment of American tourists.

But of all that great and glittering company, the Scotch barrister, parasite as he may have been, built the strongest immortality of them all. His book is the focal point of English biography. Before it appeared in 1783, many things had happened but nothing had been fixed.

There is no one's work, not even Cavendish's or Johnson's himself, of which we can say, there is the thing itself, that which was meant to be.

It is idle to discuss whether Boswell was a genius or a lucky fool. Perhaps there is little difference between the two. Walter Raleigh was content to say: "The accident which gave Boswell to Johnson and Johnson to Boswell is one of the most extraordinary pieces of good fortune in literary history." Something more than stupidity is necessary to utilize fortune when it comes one's way. It is possible to ascribe Boswell's first meeting with Johnson to luck, his later acquaintance to subservience plus a certain good fellowship and crafty parasitism on his part. Only intent could have noted down and stored away the material from which the "Life" was finally written and only genuine ability could have produced a work still so readable, still so fascinating, still so real even in this modern age, as Boswell's "Johnson."

There is one more debt which the world owes to Johnson and by the same token to Boswell. Before their time the lot of a literary man was a hard one. During his life he wore out his soul and his clothes in Grub Street, frequently subsisting literally on the crumbs that fell from rich men's tables. Ignored and sometimes starving during his life, he was usually forgotten after his death. The old English phrase about strolling players and other vagabonds might have applied equally well to gentlemen of the pen. Johnson gave them a new dignity and a new worth. His "Lives of the Poets," coupled with Mason's "Life of Gray," and followed by Boswell's "Life of Samuel Johnson" served notice on the world that hereafter it must deal seriously with the writer as a producer and a creator, a maker of history, and not a hanger-on. If that were all that these two men had done, it would still be a contribution of high merit.

VII

FRANKLIN AND GIBBON

THE eighteenth century saw still another
beginning, that of autobiography. I have said
that the seeds were sown in St. Augustine's
"Confessions." Cellini accomplished a marvel
of frankness with no imitators. It was Cellini
who stated the case for autobiography in his
opening sentence: "All men, whatever be
their condition, who have done anything of
merit, or which verily has a semblance of
merit, if so be they are men of truth and good
repute, should write the tale of their life with
their o.vn hand." Samuel Pepys achieved autobiography without intending it. Walton wrote
it between the lines of his lives of the good if
not the great. Colley Cibber added something
in "An Apology for the Life of Colley Cibber."
But Colley Cibber belonged to a profession
just becoming barely respectable and his
leadership in that profession was of doubtful
quality to everyone except himself.

Two great sons of the eighteenth century not only made a beginning in autobiography but achieved a level of performance that has seldom been approached and probably never surpassed. These two were Benjamin Franklin and Edward Gibbon. The period these two men covered was substantially the same. Gibbon lived from 1729 to 1794 and Franklin from 1706 to 1790. In all other respects, except that of time, the two men were diametrically different.

Franklin was of humble birth, ambitious, self-assured, practical, shrewd, tireless, universal in his interest; Gibbon, critical of the world, analytical of himself, was satisfied only with his monumental work on the "Decline and Fall of the Roman Empire." Franklin was in large part self-taught. He was a printer's apprentice when he was twelve, a runaway at twenty, curious about and a dabbler in practically every known branch of human knowledge, actively concerned in political affairs in the Colonies and at the end a supporter of revolution and a foreign ambassador for the government that the revolution brought into being.

Gibbon's tastes were exclusively classical and although he served a brief period in

English politics, his service was largely nominal and due to his position and the wealth of his family. Actually his interests, like his achievements, were confined to his monumental history. In spite of these wide differences between the men, both achieved something close to the perfect autobiography. Neither attempted to produce an unduly favorable picture of himself beyond achieving a considerable degree of detachment. Neither one attempted to rationalize after the fact or to justify or explain away circumstances of which they were not too proud.

Franklin's autobiography, "Memoirs of the Life and Writings of Benjamin Franklin," was published first in fragmentary form in 1817 and in its complete form in 1868. It covers only fifty-six years of a life that lasted eighty-four. Actually the most generally interesting years of his life, those in which he was actively a member of the Colonial Assembly formulating a plan for a new and powerful British empire at the Albany convention, signing the Declaration of Independence, representing the Colonies in England and later in France, signing the Treaty of Friendship with France, the Treaty of Peace with England, and the

Constitution of the United States, all belong to the later and unrecorded period of his activity.

It would not be far from the truth to characterize his autobiography as an attempt to present his practical philosophy of life. That, however, is not to write it down as a series of sermons on thrift, prudence, business success, social advancement, association with others, and kindred topics. Benjamin Franklin was no Samuel Smiles. More than any other one man he was the realist of the Revolution, as Thomas Paine was its philosopher. Until separation became obviously unavoidable he fought for union, not a union of subservience but a union of equal strength such as he outlined at Albany. His philosophy is the philosophy of a realist who saw the world objectively and interestingly, who knew that without capital no new country could prosper and who realized that capital grows only as a result of thrift and prudence.

His Poor Richard's maxims are not merely wise sayings but are the framework of conduct which he saw as necessary in the building of an enduring society and a powerful state. In that respect his maxims are an essential part of his autobiography. Inventor, scientist, philosopher, philanthropist, statesman, diplomat, everything that he did was a logical and intelligent extension of the principles laid down in his autobiography.

Two other philosophers were born at about the same time, Samuel Johnson and Jonathan Edwards. Of the three, Franklin knew more and cared more about the world in which he lived and more deeply impressed himself upon his time and the generations to follow. The printer's apprentice lived to be the most famous man in the two worlds. Two American universities and three English gave him honorary degrees. He attracted more attention in Paris than the king himself, and wealthy Parisian women sat at his feet not only metaphorically but actually. He made many inventions, wrote many pamphlets and articles, but he patented no inventions and copyrighted no books. He was active and instrumental in the founding in Philadelphia of the fire and police departments, as well as a city hospital; in paving, cleaning, and lighting the streets; and in organizing the first militia company. He was instrumental in the birth of the institution that later grew into the University of Pennsylvania, and *The Saturday Evening Post* boasts on its front cover that it was founded by Benjamin Franklin.

Here is a list of achievements sufficient to satisfy even the most ambitious. As a writer he developed, by constant practice, careful study, and the habit of close, clear thinking, a simple, direct, effective style that is as easily read and understood today as by the readers of his own time. It is as singularly free from the Latin style of his day as it is free from every other form of affectation or artificiality.

The verdict of history in the case of Benjamin Franklin as a writer has been well expressed by Paul Leicester Ford, historian and novelist: "This self-educated boy and busy, practical man gave to American literature the most popular autobiography ever written, a series of political and social satires that can bear comparison with those of the greatest satirists, a private correspondence as readable as Walpole's or Chesterfield's, and the collection of Poor Richard's epigrams, which has been oftener printed and translated than any other production of an American pen."

His account of his practice in the art of writing is a powerful example of the process of self-education. He had been reading an odd volume of *The Spectator* and was delighted with the simplicity and clearness of the writing and wished to imitate it.

"With this view I took some of the papers, and, making short hints to the sentiment in each sentence, laid them by a few days, and then, without looking at the book, try'd to compleat the papers again, by expressing each hinted sentiment at length, and as fully as it had been expressed before, in any suitable words that should come to hand. Then I compared my *Spectator* with the original, discovered some of my faults, and corrected them. But I found I wanted a stock of words, or a readiness in recollecting and using them, which I thought I should have acquired before that time if I had gone on making verses; since the continual occasion for words of the same import, but of different length, to suit the measure, or of different sound for the rhyme, would have laid me under a constant necessity of searching for variety, and also have tended to fix that variety in my mind, and make me master of it. Therefore I took some of the tales and turned them into verse; and, after a time, when I had pretty well forgotten the prose, turned them back again. I also sometimes jumbled my collection of hints into confusion, and after some weeks endeavored to reduce them into the best order, before I began to form the full sentences and compleat the paper. This was to teach method in the arrangement of thoughts. By comparing my work afterwards with the original, I discovered many faults and amended them; but I sometimes had the pleasure of fancying that, in certain particulars of small import, I had been lucky enough to improve the method or the language, and this encouraged me to think I might possibly in time come to be a tolerable English writer of which I was extremely ambitious."

Franklin's attitude toward money shown in his writings and his conduct was anything but that of a miser. No one understood better than he the place and purpose of thrift in a new country. His own words in "Poor Richard's Almanac" testify to this fact and demonstrate also the breadth and power of his everyday philosophy:

"The use of money is all the advantage there is in having money.

"For six pounds a year you may have the use of one hundred pounds, provided you are a man of known prudence and honesty.

"He that spends a groat a day idly spends idly above six pounds a year, which is the price for the use of one hundred pounds.

"He that wastes idly a groat's worth of

his time per day, one day with another, wastes the privilege of using one hundred pounds each day.

"Again, he that sells upon credit asks a price for what he sells equivalent to the principal and interest of his money for the time he is to be kept out of it; therefore he that buys upon credit pays interest for what he buys, and he that pays ready money might let that money out to use; so that he that possesses anything he has bought, pays interest for the use of it.

"Yet, in buying goods, it is best to pay ready money, because he that sells upon credit expects to lose five per cent by bad debts; therefore he charges, on all he sells upon credit, an advance that shall make up that deficiency.

"Those who pay for what they buy upon credit pay their share of this advance.

"He that pays ready money escapes, or may escape, that charge.

> "A penny saved is two pence clear,
> A pin a day's a groat a year."

These comments are not the comments of a money-lover but of an economist and of a man who thoroughly understood the corrosive effects of wastefulness in the life of a nation.

A little essay that is worth quoting entirely was one that he wrote for "Poor Richard's Almanac" in 1756; it is as much a part of his autobiography in portraying the essential man as though it were a description of his experiences rather than of the thing that gave point and power to the experience:

"As I spent some weeks last winter in visiting my old acquaintances in the Jerseys, great complaints I heard for want of money, and that leave to make more paper bills could not be obtained. Friends and countrymen, my advice on this head shall cost you nothing; and if you will not be angry with me for giving it, I promise you not to be offended if you do not take it.

"You spend yearly at least two hundred thousand pounds, it is said, in European, East Indian, and West Indian commodities. Suppose one-half of this expense to be in things absolutely necessary, the other half may be called superfluities, or, at least, conveniences, which, however, you might live without for one little year and not suffer exceedingly. Now, to save this half, observe these few directions:

"1. When you incline to have new clothes, look first well over the old ones and see if you cannot shift with them another year, either by scouring, mending, or even patching if necessary. Remember, a patch on your coat and money in your pocket is better and more creditable than a writ on your back and no money to take it off.

"2. When you are inclined to buy china-ware, chintzes, India silks, or any other of their flimsy, slight manufactures, I would not be so hard with you as to insist on your absolutely resolving against it; all I advise is to put it off (as you do your repentance) till another year, and this, in some respects, may prevent an occasion of repentance.

"3. If you are now a drinker of punch, wine, or tea twice a day, for the ensuing year drink them but once a day. If you now drink them but once a day, do it but every other day. If you do it now but once a week, reduce the practice to once a fortnight. And if you do not exceed in quantity as you lessen the times, half your expense in these articles will be saved.

"4. When you incline to drink rum, fill the glass half with water.

"Thus at the year's end there will be a hundred thousand pounds more money in your country.

"If paper money in ever so great a quantity could be made, no man could get any of it without giving something for it. But all he saves in this way will be his own for nothing, and his country actually so much richer. Then the merchants' old and doubtful debts may be honestly paid off, and trading become surer thereafter, if not so extensive."

A sample of the power of his writing when directed to a particular purpose is his letter to William Strahan, longtime London friend and after the beginning of hostilities doomed to be a national enemy:

To William Strahan
Philadelphia, 5 July, 1775.

Mr. Strahan:

You are a member of Parliament, and one of that majority which has doomed my country to destruction. You have begun to burn our towns, and murder our people. Look upon your hands; they are stained with the blood of your relations! You and I were long friends; you are now my enemy, and I am,

Yours,
B. FRANKLIN

It is characteristic of the man perhaps that in 1728, at the age of twenty-two, he wrote an epitaph which he desired to be graven on his tomb. Naturally it is here presented more

as a sample of his skill with words than as any
expression of a permanent desire on his part
destined to be carried out after his death:

Epitaph Written in 1728
The Body
of
Benjamin Franklin
Printer
(Like the cover of an old book
Its contents torn out
And stript of its lettering and gilding)
Lies here, food for worms.
But the work shall not be lost
For it will (as he believed) appear once more
In a new and more elegant edition
Revised and corrected
by
The Author.

Edward Gibbon was, as I have said, the son
of a wealthy family destined for the life of
educated leisure peculiar to English families
of that rank in the eighteenth century. He was
entered at Magdalen College at Oxford at the
age of fifteen and spent an unsatisfactory
fourteen months. In "The Autobiography of
Edward Gibbon" he says of this period: "To
the University of Oxford I acknowledge no
obligation; and she will as cheerfully renounce
me for a son, as I am willing to disclaim her for

a mother. I spent fourteen months at Magdalen College; they proved the fourteen months the most idle and unprofitable of my whole life."

He has little that is good to say of the Oxford colleges of his time and no praise for the tutors, his own or any others. In fact, his memory of Oxford seemed to be merely that of a place in which to grow old at the expense of a moss-grown, unstimulating, uninteresting foundation. For a time in his Oxford career he coquetted with Catholicism and even declared his conversion. Because of this and his generally unsatisfactory performance with his tutors he was sent by his father to Lausanne where he lived in the family of a Calvinist minister and fell in love with the minister's daughter. The match was broken off by his father without apparently causing great grief to either young Gibbon or Mlle. Curchod. Gibbon says of this episode in his life in his autobiography: "After a painful struggle, I yielded to my fate; I sighed as a lover, I obeyed as a son; my wound was insensibly healed by time, absence, and the habits of a new life. My cure was accelerated by a faithful report of the tranquility and cheerfulness of the lady herself, and my love subsided in friendship and esteem."

The young lady too found comfort not in philosophy but in a successful marriage with Monsieur Necker, Treasurer General of France. The Lausanne experience and the enforced separation from Mlle. Curchod seems to have improved his relationship with his father, which had been strained, to state it mildly. At any rate, on meeting after a separation of five years he says of his father: "He received me as a man and a friend: . . . and we ever afterwards continued on the same terms of easy and equal politeness."

Gibbon's history of the "Decline and Fall of the Roman Empire" was written from 1776 to 1788 and with the autobiography is the full fruit of his work. Readers of history are familiar with his style, stately, frequently sonorous with ponderous figures of speech. But he was capable of great clarity too. The passage in which he describes the birth of the idea of the "Decline and Fall" illustrates this quality: "It was at Rome on the 15th of October, 1754, as I sat musing amidst the ruins of the Capitol while the barefooted friars were singing vespers in the temple of Jupiter, that the idea of writing the decline and fall of the city first started to my mind."

In spite of the nearly one hundred and fifty years that have passed since the completion of his work, there is little to add to it as a careful, unbiased, thorough-going presentation of a great subject. As he makes clear in his autobiography, he sought to trace the course and causes of the downfall of the great structure of Rome by showing the process of events in order as they occured. There are few hypotheses or assumptions, no illusions, and few prejudices.

Aside from his historical work there is little to be said of Gibbon's career. During his short period in the House of Commons he was a staunch supporter of George III and Lord North, although it is difficult to discover from his writing that he was even aware of the Revolution that was brewing across the Atlantic in which Franklin was playing so strong a part. One of his comments illustrates his attitude: "The cause of government was ably vindicated by Lord North, a statesman of spotless integrity, a consummate master of debate, etc. . . . "

There were a few fair autobiographies before Franklin and Gibbon. There have been many since written by big men and by small. Many have dealt frankly with the habits, the achievements, the virtues, the sins of the writers.

None, however, except perhaps "The Education of Henry Adams," has presented, through the direct evidence of documents and the implied evidence between the lines, any clearer, fuller or more interesting pictures of the lives portrayed than have Franklin and Gibbon.

One of the hectic dreamlike figures of the eighteenth century who has left himself on record is Jean Jacques Rousseau. The son of a Geneva watchmaker, physical weakling from birth, shy, sensual, sensitive, his shrill part in the tumult of the times combined to make of him one of the stormy petrels of the Revolution. His "Confessions," published in 1782 and 1789, would be entitled to rank high among autobiographical writing if the man himself possessed a larger share of adirmable qualities. The fact that he has not attempted to gloss over his weaknesses has turned his "Confessions" into more of a documentation of abnormal psychology than most readers admire. This may amount to saying that if the autobiography were less truthful it would be more admired.

Perhaps the difficulty with poor Jean Jacques is not so much that in his weaknesses he was worse than many other men but that his weaknesses filled so much of his life that he had little else to describe. Even those writings in which he sought to paint a better world, "Émile" and "Contrat Social," have neither the robustness nor the wisdom to compensate for the hectic aura that surrounded the writer during most of his life.

Nevertheless, his "Confessions" are entitled to that respect which belongs to honest work. Whatever his shortcomings he told the truth about himself. From his youthful love affairs, which are described with considerable restraint, through all the tribulations of his tumultuous life, the curious, half-boyish, half-roué affair with Madame de Warens, the really emotional peak of his experiences, down to the very end of his days, it is all there. He hated injustice and that hatred colored most of his writing. But in his "Confessions" he admits a still more burning hatred of superiority, of strength, of position, of wealth, of expectation. He confesses to his petty vices of thievery, of sensuality, of miserliness. In Turin he studied for the priesthood, not from any expectation of genuine spiritual service or in a spirit of exaltation, but because he thought he saw in the church a comfortable haven.

He indulged in a brief dream of martial glory and admits with a kind of rueful amusement that his physical weakness and lack of courage rendered the career of a soldier impossible. He steals a ribbon from the mistress of the house in which he lives and explains its presence in his room by saying that a maid gave it to him. He undertook to teach music, knowing nothing of the technique of the art, and remarks with a self-satisfied air: "By continuing to teach music I insensibly gained some knowledge of it."

He understood himself much better than most egotists and found considerable satisfaction in revealing this understanding. "A continual wish to unbosom myself puts my heart perpetually on my lips." Of course, he was usually unaware that the self that he desired to unbosom was frequently a small, mean, unworthy self. In all his contacts and experiences it was Jean Jacques Rousseau who was of supreme importance to him. He flatters himself that his love affair with Madame de Warens, sincere as it apparently was, was also an appropriate gesture of appreciation of her kindness to him.

The daily effort of his life was to devise ways and means by which he might live as comfortably as might be at the expense of others. And with the exception of his curious attitude toward Madame de Warens, he expresses little gratitude for the charity that he experienced most of his life.

To find in Rousseau's "Confessions" any evidence of a sincere social interest, of a genuine desire to improve mankind, is not easy. His attitude even in the most objective of his writings remains highly personal and he declares that the opposition which "Contrat Social" and "Émile" aroused was the result of jealousy and was not directed against anything in his books. Perhaps the highest point of irony that he touches is in his declaration that the criticism he receives is and must remain a mystery to him.

If there is such a thing as psychological biography, Jean Jacques Rousseau should attract and receive the attention of some competent practitioner of that elusive art.

VIII

THE MYSTERY OF WASHINGTON

IN A discussion of biography necessarily so
brief as this one, there is constant temptation
to abridge the treatment of any one individual
beyond that figure's reasonable demands. In
the case of one so much discussed, maligned,
and overpraised as George Washington, the
drawing of the line is doubly difficult. As long
ago as 1899 W. S. Baker in his "Bibliotheca
Washingtoniana" listed 502 works that were
in his judgment entitled to be called lives of
Washington. Most of these have long since
fallen into the oblivion that they deserved.
Perhaps the really great "life" of Washington
has not yet been written. Possibly none will
be written until writers have forgotten to be
controversialists or crusaders or pamphleteers
or at least have learned to write with a little
blissful forgetfulness of the work of others
with whom they too completely and violently
disagree.

In any discussion of the lives of George
Washington first place belongs to Mason

Locke Weems. The first edition of his work appeared in 1800, a year after Washington's death, and each of the next eleven years saw a new edition published. Eighty in all have appeared from 1800 to 1930.

It is hardly worth while to discuss Parson Weems seriously as a biographer, although perhaps it is only fair to remark that considering how badly he might have done, the marvel is that he did as well as the record shows. Such praise, however, is a little like praising a trained seal for its piano playing. In the case of the seal the result is surprising but certainly not music. In the case of Weems the result has been both surprising and long-lived, although assuredly not biography. We have Weems to thank for the whole galaxy of incident, argument, and general prevarication and misrepresentation which began the embalming of Washington in our memories. That he should be preserved to us in any aspect other than as a marble figure is matter for wonder.

Weems was a typical character of his time, itinerant peddler, preacher, pamphleteer, a picker up and user of unconsidered trifles. He misrepresented even himself, claiming to have been the rector of Mt. Vernon parish although there was no such parish and no such church. Washington's church was in Alexandria, where visitors are still shown his pew. There is no evidence that Weems was even an Episcopalian or in fact that he was a member in good standing of any recognized denomination. In view of all his disabilities it is surprising that he came as near as he did to presenting a fairly interesting and in places authentic account not only of Washington but of the Revolutionary campaigns in which Washington took part. The reason presumably is that at the time in which he wrote, these campaigns were still vivid in men's memories and information about them was part of the current material of conversation, gossip, and reminiscence in the taverns and village streets and country homes which Weems seems to have frequented.

From the beginning Washington suffered more at the hands of his friends than of his enemies. In 1834 to 1838 and 1844 to 1848 Jared Sparks, Professor of History and President of Harvard University, biographer of John Ledyard and of Gouverneur Morris, produced a Library of American Biography in two series and twenty-five volumes, a monument of research but containing little critical illumination. He was also the editor of the collected writings of Washington in twelve volumes, and of Franklin in ten volumes. The verbosity and smugness of his biographies may be pardoned or overlooked, but his work as editor of the letters of these two great Americans is not so easily forgotten. To him we are indebted not only for the omission of important letters or parts of letters but also the altering of phraseology. Phrases that seemed to the good Dr. Sparks unduly violent or otherwise inappropriate to the picture of the great and good Washington that he had elected to present were modified or omitted altogether.

To Washington Irving more praise may be given, although, when he wrote his five-volume life of the great man in 1855 to 1859, it was still dangerous to present the reality of the great original on the printed page. Irving was first of all a conscientious literary gentleman rather than a biographer or historian. Social practices, backgrounds, and personal relationships interested him more than facts of character or motive.

Justice Marshall's five-volume "Washington" is useful but not a biography. The second volume is well under way before the infant Washington appears and the chief justice was more concerned with certain things that happened after the first president's death than with the events and immediate meanings of his life.

With such characters as Washington the chronological method offers little aid. He cast too deep a shadow on his own time. He was too much praised, too much hated, too much feared, to be understood. We are only now nearing the point, if even yet, when we may be able to offer a correct appraisal. Many have tried it in recent years. Norman Hapgood's "Washington" is correct but un-illuminating. W. E. Woodward presents an appealing picture of a Virginia gentleman in "George Washington, the Image and the Man," but too much the gentleman and not enough the patriot farmer. Owen Wister has drawn "The Seven Ages of Washington," but Washington is more than a subject for historical sermons. Shelby Little has written a "George Washington" that is easily read and as easily forgotten. Worthington C. Ford has done the best work of all in his edition of Washington's letters and papers, and his brother, Paul Leicester Ford, presents an interesting figure in "The True George Washington," although such titles usually arouse suspicion. The task is longer and more difficult and requires more critical and historical insight than our rapid-fire journalists have realized.

Perhaps the most significant thing that has yet been done is Rupert Hughes's "George Washington." How far we have traveled since the days of Weems can be determined by reading Mr. Hughes's characterization of Washington as a "big, blundering, bewildered giant." And even today to many devotees the noun hardly atones for the sacrilege of the adjectives. The discriminating reader of Mr. Hughes is not yet prepared to say: "Here is Washington." It is too controversial, too angry, perhaps too cocksure. But with all its anger and cocksureness, a human figure appears. Let Mr. Hughes state his own case: "It is poor patriotism, ridiculous idolatry, and rank dishonesty to rob the host of other strugglers for liberty and progress of their just deserts and to perpetuate old slanders against his enemies at home and abroad in order to turn Washington into a god. As a god, Washington was a woeful failure; as a man he was tremendous. This is a study of the man."

Here we see at least a human Washington, fond of dress, devoted to dancing, to fox hunting, the theater, the card table. His diary shows that in 1770 in Williamsburg, Virginia, he attended five plays in seven days. Extracts from the same source reveal that his success at cards was not in keeping with his interest. A careful record of winnings and losses shows losses predominating. There are in his diaries and letters references to fair ladies, some long since forgotten, others whose names are still faint echoes—the "Lowland Beauty," Mary Cary, Sally Fairfax, Mary Philipse. Evidently the young George, and later on the not so young George, properly characterized himself a "votary of love."

On many pages Mr. Hughes reveals the fact that he is too anxious to make a case to be a genuine biographer. He is too sweeping in his assertions, too violent in his denunciation. Also there appears from time to time too much inclination to bridge a gap of evidence with a "perhaps" or a "possibly," as in such phrases as: "He may have thought"; "She must have said"; "It may have been." Imagination is valuable to the biographer, but not if it is used as a substitute for evidence. An illustration is in Mr. Hughes's reference to the captors of Major André: "Opinion at the time varied as to whether these three men were incorruptible patriots or mercenary blackguards. They were probably the latter, but being unable to figure out how to sell André to the British safely, turned him over to Colonel Jameson at Armonk." It is hardly the business of the cautious or reliable biographer to venture so far into the realm of fiction as this sample suggests.

In spite of all its faults of temper and haste, in spite of a tendency to argue where argument is dangerous or unnecessary, in spite also of a frequently turgid style, Hughes presents a human Washington—farmer, tobacco grower, hunter, fisherman, stock-breeder, racing enthusiast, real-estate speculator, and country gentleman. He proves him lacking in introspection, with no powers of self-analysis and with no conviction of sin. Late in life Washington is alleged to have said something like this: "I have never said anything or written anything that I cared to recall nor ever done anything that I regretted." So George Washington told Louis Philippe, who told the Duc d'Aumale, who told Chauncey M. Depew, who told Norman Hapgood, who wrote it in his life of Washington.

Nevertheless, whatever he was, let it not be forgotten that George Washington led the armies of the Colonies through a disastrous and losing war at great risk to himself, without hope of profit, and in great danger of the scaffold if he were captured. Without political sagacity, interest, or ambition, he was President of the United States for eight difficult years, probably suffering more during that time than any human being ever suffered in such exalted station. Nowhere in all of the five or six hundred books written about him, the thousands of magazine articles or tens of thousands of speeches for and against him, has there been at any time a credible hint of an act, public or private, that involved any stain whatever on his character or any reflection on his great integrity. And the man who did these things was a Virginia planter, a farmer, concerned over the restoration of his worn-out fields, the state of the tobacco market, and the health of his slaves. No one who forgets these facts can ever write a successful history of George Washington. Perhaps the task can be done only by a combination of Henry Adams, Gamaliel Bradford, and Stephen Vincent Benét.

IX

THE GREAT CENTURY

WE COME now to a great period in English history, a period of marked activity in politics, in literature, in social changes and reforms, and of great interest in human beings. But it must be said that in spite of the brave beginning by such men as Boswell, Gibbon, Franklin, for a long time there was a period of sterility in the field of biography. Nicolson dismisses the first half of the reign of Victoria as a period of moral earnestness, a quality that in his view spreads an inescapable blight over all biography. Perhaps the French Revolution had frightened England and English thinkers more than England knew. After all, the European world had come close to the edge of a rather forbidding abyss and for at least a generation after the Battle of Waterloo, England was constantly in danger of retreating in horror from steps which she would have taken normally with little thought or fear. The Whig party, which had in its ranks some of the most powerful thinkers and greatest patriots, suffered from the unavoidable implications of the Revolution.

One result of this national state of mind was an overappreciation of easily understood and expressed moral qualities. Compare, for example, the "Life of Arnold" by Arthur Penryhn Stanley and the one produced by Lytton Strachey in his "Eminent Victorians." Stanley wrote in a heat of enthusiasm for and devotion to his greatest of schoolmasters. He was but lately removed from the spell of the physical presence of the great man. He was still in awe of the memory of the reforms that Arnold had instituted at Rugby and the better spirit that he had spread through the whole public-school field. Judging by the difficulty with which the modern reader struggles through his stumbling sentences, it must have been a difficult book to write. It is certainly difficult enough to read in its lack of proper arrangement, its overcrowding with unimportant details, and its awkward mixture of fact, illustration, comment, and highly favorable judgment. To crown it all, the writer asks the reader to wade through the good doctor's letters, confined in a separate section without explanation or notation. Of course, the result is that no one except the thick and thin adherents of Arnold read the letters, and the light that they might have shed on a proper understanding of this really great headmaster is quite lost.

Strachey, on the other hand, does less than justice to Arnold, as he does also to "Chinese" Gordon and Florence Nightingale. Of course, to Strachey the stiff, formal piety of Arnold, the hard-boiled, vinegarish persistence of Miss Nightingale, the half-heroic, half-alcoholic zeal of Gordon are all curiously characteristic of the Victorian era and for that reason doubly to be hated. It is not clear whether Strachey disliked these qualities in these unlucky souls because they were Victorian—and he hated all things Victorian—or hated things Victorian because he found in Victorians an abundance of these qualities. In any event the result is the same.

But Stanley's blind zeal and Strachey's too keen-eyed cynicism are both unable to quite conceal the fact that Thomas Arnold found Rugby a sink of petty vice, of mean tyranny on the part of masters and older boys, of wretched living and still more wretched instruction and that in thirteen years he left it one of the great public schools of England. This

he did almost singlehanded. Had he been a
different person he might still have done it.
But the fact to be considered is that, being
what he was, he still did what he did and
neither Stanley nor Strachey has done all
that might be done for Arnold. These two
men and what they wrote are entitled to so
much space here because to both of them
Arnold represented the high point of Victorian
moral earnestness—to Stanley a quality never
sufficiently to be praised and to Strachey a
weakness never enough condemned.

Whether or not, as Nicolson insists, it was
the moral earnestness of Thomas Arnold,
particularly as reflected in Stanley's biography, which infected the whole nation and
made of English biography a weak and puny
thing until Froude cleared the air with his
"Life of Carlyle," it is nevertheless true that
from early in the century to the early eighties,
with one or two exceptions, there are few
names of great significance.

Much of the biographical writing at any
time is, of course, unrelated to intellectual
movements or to any other general current
of interest or of activity. Walter Scott, early
in his career, became a biographer with his

"Life of Dryden," which is an attempt at a critical appreciation of Dryden, but tends actually to become more a detailed picture of the background and life of Dryden's time.

Robert Southey rose to the occasion after Trafalgar with a "Life of Nelson" which the modern critic disposes of as unscholarly, inadequate, and written wholly for the sake of praising the great admiral, all of which is true. England had not yet recovered from the French and particularly the Napoleonic menace. The man who broke the power of Villeneuve at Trafalgar brought the blessing of security to the channel ports, and when Nelson died on the deck of the *Victory* there passed a man whose service could never be repaid. Of course, Southey's book is a panegyric. Of course, he ignores Lady Hamilton. Probably Lady Hamilton deserved to be ignored. What Southey wrote and what he meant to write was a combination of a tribute to a national hero and a kind of spiritual handbook and manual for young Englishmen, particularly those looking forward to service in the navy. It is not a great biography in any respect. It is not even a good biography, but it is an extremely useful milestone in the history of English biography and an excellent index to the English state of mind at the time when this book was written.

William Godwin deserves to be remembered for his "Life of Chaucer" written early in the century (1803), if for no other reason than because Professor Lounsbury of Yale declared it "the most worthless piece of biography in the English language." This is remarkable if true.

A disappointment to admirers of the two poets was Thomas Moore's "Life of Lord Byron" (1830). There was every reason for expecting a great book. Moore was himself a poet, sympathetic and friendly with Byron but by taste and inclination in his own method qualified to stand out and justly to weigh and appraise. He had been a frequent correspondent with Byron and had access to tremendous quantities of letters, journals, and notes. He visited Byron twice at Venice, and on the second occasion in 1821 received the manuscript of the greater poet's journal with instructions to publish it after the writer's death. This manuscript was burned unpublished at the request of Byron's relatives, an example of the delicate decency of English biography which Carlyle denounced.

Possibly there was too much material. Probably the Byron controversy was still too hot. Perhaps Moore attempted to please both friends and enemies instead of only himself. At any rate, the general result is a vast mass of material badly arranged and incoherent as to its implications. Whatever the reason it can be said that Thomas Moore turned a great opportunity into something dangerously near a failure. Because of its failures and inadequacies, it is easily possible to underestimate the importance of this period. During this time there was a marked growth in readers' interest in biography. In other words the market began to appear. Spedding's "Life of Bacon" saw the light at this time, also Masson's "Milton" and Lewes's "Goethe." It was in this period that the series of "English Men of Letters" began to appear under the able although conventional and not particularly inspiring editorship of Leslie Stephen. The Dictionary of National Biography in England was established, and the writing of biography took a distinctly professional turn which it has not yet lost.

An example of the careful, painstaking, scholarly and uninspired and uninspiring work of this time is George Henry Lewes's "Life of Goethe." Probably the equation was an impossible one from the beginning. At any rate, as the world sees Goethe today it is inconceivable that a man like Lewes should even have attempted to understand, much less to describe him. Those episodes in Goethe's life which were least creditable to him, chiefly his love affairs, are ignored or explained away as of only passing importance. The modern biographer sees in them sure indices of an important phase of Goethe's character reflected more than once in his writing. Lewes's philosophy was a combination of the old, somewhat agreeable teleological arguments colored by the early stages of the evolutionary hypothesis then beginning to be discussed. The year in which Lewes's "Goethe" appeared was 1855.

Another weakness which Lewes betrays is the attempt to find for Goethe a singularity of reaction to environment or experience denied to other men of his time. This involves him in a tacit denial of unusual powers of personality in Goethe, which leaves him only one of the rank and file. For example, he cites the destruction of life and property in the Lisbon earthquake as affecting

Goethe's religious faith. The result is that
Mr. Lewes is unfortunately in danger of explaining Goethe in a half-baked approximation
of the modern psychological manner without
succeeding either in this attempt or in presenting a genuine genius driven by the power which
originated within himself. He offers an excellent picture of life in Weimar, the small, crude,
placid, ignorant German capital, and is skillful
in holding all of his pictures to the scale of
Weimar life. To be sure, his absorption in the
details of Weimar leads him to argue overmuch
on the effect of court life on Goethe's work.
Other evidence suggests that the poet was
little affected by Weimar and held his court
responsibility in low esteem.

Lewes's tendency to rationalize Goethe,
to present the brilliant, irresponsible poet,
artist, dreamer, in the terms of Lewes's own
life and concepts, tends unfortunately to
bring the German bad boy and genius down
to the dimensions of middle-class England.
He is constantly on the verge of presenting
an excellent impression of the gloom and
sentimentality that overspread much of Ger-
many in Goethe's time. But as the picture
is about to grow to credible dimensions, his

fear of British respectability leads him to bowdlerize it almost out of recognition.

It is too bad that Carlyle did not carry out his oft expressed intention to write a life of Goethe to follow up his translations and critical articles on the work of the poet. There is reason to believe that had he done so not only would Lewes's "Goethe" have disappeared but there would have been less reason to grieve over Carlyle's rather commonplace "Life of Schiller."

X

SCOTT AND BRONTË

It is not difficult to put one's finger on the outstanding biography of the early half of the nineteenth century. In spite of criticism, praise, and argument, that still remains the "Memoirs of the Life of Sir Walter Scott," by J. G. Lockhart. Lockhart, like Roper, was actuated partly by filial affection. He was the son-in-law of the novelist, a close associate, and a sincere admirer. Unlike Roper, he was himself a trained writer, a hard-working student of men and affairs, and unflinching in his sense of fidelity to the canons of his art. His life of Napoleon is by no means the worst that has been done for that great enigma.

In the case of Scott there was no occasion for justification. The great Sir Walter has come today into that place least to be desired by the writer. He is known as the author of books which everybody praises and no one reads. But in his time and in the time of Lockhart he was a giant bestriding the English-reading world. His Scotch novels uncovered a mine of literary treasure unknown south of the Tweed and to read his historical novels was equivalent to a thorough course in Scottish history as well as in domestic manners and, to a less extent, domestic morals. Unfortunately, somewhere he lacked the touch of immortality. When Lockhart wrote the sun of his fame was still high and shining; no one could plead ignorance and few dared plead indifference.

The temptation not to criticize Lockhart is strong. There would be no injustice in dismissing him with the verdict that considering the opportunities for error, omission and over-emphasis that his relationship gave him, it was a marvel that he erred so little. The sanest criticism that can be leveled against his biography is that it is too long and too heavy. He followed the model of Boswell in letting his subject tell his own story so far as possible in letter, in conversation, and in incident. Unfortunately, fascinating actor as he was on the stage of his time, the Scott personal performance lacked the enduring quality that Samuel Johnson all unknown possessed. Probably Scott's performance was a little self-conscious and insincere. He loved too well the

self-assumed role of Scottish laird, baron
of the border. To be painted with his favorite
dog was not to him a minor incident but a
rite and a duty which he owed to posterity.
He wrote with a shade too much of exaltation
and appreciation of what different noblemen
had said to him and how that lady of title
had curtsied deep on meeting him. He never
quite overcame the simple awe he felt at
discovering in himself the ability to impress
not only his Scotch neighbors but the alien
English. If the truth were known it is probable
that Sir Walter impressed the alien English
far more than he did his Scotch neighbors.

Lockhart's "Life" may be, as I have said,
heavy and dull, but the material is all there.
If the occasion demanded, it would be possible
for the biographer of today to produce a classic
living picture of the great man and never step
once outside the chapters of Lockhart for
his material.

Nicolson sneers mildly at Lockhart's "Life"
as impressionistic rather than narrative. Perhaps, but it is probably equally true that if
any name has yet appeared which deserves
to be written next to that of James Boswell
it is Lockhart. The much-quoted passage
in which he describes the death of Scott is

certainly impressive, whether narrative or impressionistic: "'Lockhart,' he said, 'I may have but a minute to speak to you. My dear, be a good man—be virtuous—be religious—be a good man. Nothing else will give you any comfort when you come to lie here.'"

Recently a capable novelist, John Buchan, has attempted the resurrection of Scott. It is to be doubted if the temperament of the novelist lends itself to the writing of biography. Mr. Buchan has tried hard, he knows the Scotch, he has excellent standards of literary performance, but his Sir Walter remains a shadowy actor on a dim and distant stage. Biography and fiction are related but different arts.

The gap can be bridged and occasionally is. A case in point is one of the later biographical performances, E. F. Benson's "Charlotte Brontë." Its chief weakness lies in the fact, too obvious throughout, that Mr. Benson's chief reason for writing is to confound the first and great biographer of Miss Brontë, Mrs. Gaskell, another novelist. Mrs. Gaskell's "Life of Charlotte Brontë" has for the most part been accepted hitherto as an authentic, usually accurate, and entirely fair portrayal of the great woman novelist of the Victorian time. To be sure, by modern standards she was hardly qualified for such a task. She was a sympathetic, admiring friend, who wrote at close range of a kindred spirit perplexed in many ways by similar problems, doubts, and handicaps. It is only in our time that this state of affairs would be held to constitute a disability. In fact, in the time in which Charlotte lived and Mrs. Gaskell wrote of her, friendship, sympathy, contemporary experience were all held to be superior qualifications for such authorship, if not, in fact, the only desirable and reliable qualifications.

It is to Mrs. Gaskell that we owe the picture of Miss Brontë as in part the victim of an unfeeling, erratic, and at times cruel father and at most times of a drunken brother. Mrs. Gaskell has shown us Charlotte with her sister, lonesome, unhappy, and unappreciated in the girls' school in Brussels, first as a pupil and then as a teacher. It is to Mrs. Gaskell's pen that we are indebted for the account of the hardships of the Brontë sisters in the school at Cowan Bridge and the long struggles through which they passed to such success as was theirs. Then appears Mr. Benson, having had access to the Brontë letters in the Clement Shorter collection, to offer direct contradiction of many of the statements which contribute to build the pathetic, frequently tragic, always moving story of the Brontës.

To begin with, there is the account of the father's aristocratic Irish pedigree. Mrs. Gaskell implies that the Brontës trace their line from an old Irish family antedating the Cromwellian occupation of Ireland but in Victorian times fallen upon evil days. Mr. Benson assembles evidence that the father's father was an Irish peasant farmer, Brunty by name, and implies that the later spelling was suggested by the accident of Nelson's being made Duke of Brontë in 1799. The discovery of an aristocratic pedigree is an amiable and almost universal weakness and it is probable that most such lines have a peasant origin nearer than most genealogists or ancestor worshipers would be willing to admit. The case against Mrs. Gaskell, however, is somewhat stronger in other and more specific respects.

The picture of Patrick Brontë, the father, as cruel, at times as insane, tyrannizing over his family, forcing them to live on potatoes for days on end, carrying a loaded pistol about the house, and otherwise behaving

like a madman with a sadistic tendency, is
frequently contradicted by the testimony
of Brontë servants who were in the family for
years. Mrs. Gaskell's material on this point
seems to have been drawn largely from a
discharged servant who had been a member
of the household for a comparatively short
time. There is abundant evidence that the
father was of a hot temper, subject to moods
of depression, tortured through many years by
the fear of blindness, and broken in spirit
by the early death of his wife. But that his
attitude toward the family was in any material respect different from that of thousands
of other parents afflicted with poverty and
depressed by sorrow rests only on the evidence
of Mrs. Gaskell.

The drunkenness of Bramwell, the brother,
is another favorite theme of Mrs. Gaskell.
As a matter of fact, Mr. Benson shows that a
literal acceptance of the Gaskell record on
this point makes Bramwell a confirmed drunkard at the age of fourteen. Drunkard he
was at the end of his life, but before that
tragedy came there were several years in
which his association with his sisters appears
to have been of the most agreeable sort,
clouded only by his own thwarted ambition,

his lack of agreeable companionship of his own age, and a vague and futile process of experiment in several fields of intellectual effort.

Mr. Benson pays his respects to Mrs. Gaskell's account of the writing of the sisters, particularly of Charlotte, and rather cruelly makes literal calculation from one of Mrs. Gaskell's statements. This process shows that according to Mrs. Gaskell, Charlotte's youthful unpublished writing over a period of fifteen months must have amounted to more than two and one-quarter million words, equaling in volume approximately twenty-two modern novels.

Mrs. Gaskell makes considerable use of the overshadowing influence of the school at Cowan Bridge, which all of the Brontë sisters attended as children. She pictures the school as swept by a typhus epidemic. According to Mr. Benson the records show that only one girl died as a result of the illness and that the cause was probably influenza.

But it is in the Brussels period that Mr. Benson is most destructive of the Gaskell structure. The facts of the Brussels experience, according to Mr. Benson, are that Charlotte Brontë fell deeply in love with Monsieur

Heger, and that her apparently unwilling return to Brussels the second time, this time as a teacher, was due entirely to her feeling for the master of the school and her desire to be with him. Mr. Benson quotes from letters in the Shorter collection which can be read only as love letters and cites evidence to the effect that the recipient of these letters replied briefly and coldly and only through his wife as amanuensis. As a matter of fact, the Brontë letters which were preserved were saved by Madame Heger who rescued them from a wastebasket where Heger had thrown them. The most damaging aspect of this part of Mr. Benson's discussion is in the evidence that Mrs. Gaskell had access to some of these very letters in Brussels and quoted carefully selected passages in cases where a reproduction of the entire letter would have put an entirely different face on Charlotte's attitude toward the school and the headmaster.

The most complete proof of Mrs. Gaskell's overenthusiastic advocacy of Charlotte Brontë is in the fact that several of her statements, notably those about the father and about the school at Cowan Bridge, were eliminated or altered in a later edition of the "Life." Unfortunately for Monsieur Heger there was no one to speak so firmly for him and the Brussels experience as portrayed by Mrs. Gaskell, and Charlotte herself in her novel, "Villette," remains substantially as first presented.

In spite, however, of Mr. Benson's destructive criticism of Mrs. Gaskell, Charlotte Brontë emerges from his book rather more vivid, compelling, and unusual than from the pages of the too kindly friend. The friend's effort is apparently directed toward a justification where no justification was needed and toward an explanation which tended logically to reduce erratic genius to the dead level of ordinary talent. It is a fair assumption that the picture of Charlotte Brontë presented by Mrs. Gaskell as an abused, misunderstood, tortured spirit, beating her wings against the bars of poverty and cruelty, is largely one that the egoistic Charlotte herself presented.

Throughout her life she lived in two worlds, one the rather sordid, dull, empty world of the Haworth parsonage and the moors that surrounded the village; the other the highly colored, exciting, stimulating world of her imagination. The characters and to a considerable extent the events of her novels were drawn out of the everyday life in which she lived. But the plots, particularly the major episodes and relationships, were often those of the dream world. The result was frequently a powerful, realistic clothing draped on an absurd melodramatic frame, as in the case of "Jane Eyre."

The amiable, unsophisticated, ambitious Jane about to be married to a man already handicapped with a mad wife is undoubtedly Charlotte herself as she liked to conceive herself. The basic incident of "Jane Eyre," the finding of the unknown cousin living in the lone house on the moors to which she wanders in the typical stage storm of the Victorian novel, the fortune of which they tell her, the burning house in which the mad wife is consumed, the blind Rochester, the marriage and Rochester's surprising and miraculous recovery of his eyesight, all these are the rankest melodrama and quite characteristic of the writing of such a suppressed, unsophisticated, imaginative character as Charlotte Brontë was.

To accept Mr. Benson's conclusions rather than those of Mrs. Gaskell is to conceive of Charlotte Brontë as something near a genius instead of a rather commonplace, mildly talented, hard working, misunderstood, mistreated mid-Victorian lady.

Parenthetically, the reader of "Jane Eyre" and "Villette" would probably be willing to agree that, if the spirit of Charlotte could be asked to select which of these two pictures most pleased her egotistic soul, it would be Benson's and not Mrs. Gaskell's that would receive the award.

XI

THE PROFESSIONAL APPEARS

A STUDENT of different Victorian periods of
biography is constantly tempted to over-
criticism, perhaps to the setting of standards
that can not fairly be applied to contemporary
writing. One man who invites such treatment
is John Forster, whose "Life of Charles
Dickens" is standard for the time and is also
a favorite source for those who wish to know
something of the great caricaturist. Here
again, as in the case of Mrs. Gaskell, the
accident of friendship, of close association,
of sympathetic relationship, has operated
against rather than in favor of that compre-
hensive understanding and historical accuracy
that are necessary to proper biographical
treatment.

John Forster was a professional writer. In
fact he might be called the first professional
biographer in that he was the first man to
make in any sense a profession of the study
of other men's lives. Besides Dickens he wrote

lives of Goldsmith, Swift, and Landor. As a writer he was competent, industrious, and in obvious matters of dates, places, actions, and the external world generally, scrupulously exact. His "Life of Dickens" is a model of what might be called internal documentation. He knew his subject thoroughly and could cite chapter and verse not only from the records of letters, diaries, contracts, records of conversation, but from his knowledge of his subject's inner processes. For the last reason he betrays himself into assumptions or conclusions that are unnecessary, and deductions from the facts which might better be left to the reader. He relies overmuch on his own high opinion of Dickens, which often leads him to the citing of such incidents as would, if given in proper detail, in themselves illustrate Dickens's methods and problems far more vividly than do Forster's generalizations.

It is perhaps not quite fair to criticize Mr. Forster for his lack of perspective. It is impossible for a contemporary to see his subject down a lengthening avenue of time and correspondingly difficult for him to realize that it is down precisely such an avenue that his book will be read if it has the good fortune to live more than half a score of years.

Mr. Forster quite fails to realize that certain
of his casual references are today lacking
in importance or reality for the modern
reader. How many except the detailed student
of the Victorian era could immediately give
even the most shadowy body to the names of
Macready, Maclise, Jerrold, Beard, Talfourd,
the "Painter of 'Rent Day,'" and Stanfield,
to mention only a few. One thing that Mr.
Forster's "Life" sadly needs if it is to be
made helpful to the modern reader is a careful
annotating.

Another fault is a too high emphasis on his
own part in the Dickens's panorama. To be
sure it was to his role of friend, adviser, and
guide that he owed his extremely intimate
knowledge of the novelist's life. But while the
reader is prepared to admit that Mr. Forster
played as large a part as he implies, it is a little
wearisome to find one's self passing over a
constant succession of such phrases as "we
both laughed," "who shared with us," "whom
we visited," "that dear friend of his and
mine." His sense of kinship leads him at times
to intrude himself with no obvious reason for
the intrusion. For example, a concluding
phrase in his description of sports at Twicken-
ham in which Dickens was greatly interested

reads thus: "from the more difficult forms of which I in general modestly retired." What of it!

Incidentally, Mr. Forster claims credit for the death of Little Nell in the last chapter of the "Old Curiosity Shop." A letter that he quotes from Dickens reads: "When I first began, *on your valued suggestion*," etc. Perhaps had Mr. Forster realized how ribald and irreverent generations would look upon such literature as the death of Little Nell, he might have been slower to claim credit for his suggestion.

Forster's failure to recognize the inadequacy of his allusions and references leaves the reader speculating on several points. There are many references, for example, to arguments with publishers over contracts, casual allusions to unsatisfactory terms, but little enlargement and no indication of an understanding that in half a century or less the conditions of publishing would be so altered that most of his references would be blind and unilluminating.

There are other instances, for example, in the infrequent and usually tantalizing intimations of the manner in which ideas came to Dickens and of the formation and direction of their growth. Almost without exception such references are too vague for us to reach a more definite conclusion than that the novelist in most cases began his writing with a rather loose group of characters or a general situation in mind, the situation being an involved one or the implied character being of a quaint or whimsical or unpleasant sort, and that the plot developed out of character and situation as he wrote. This is at least a conclusion which is commonly held. So far as Mr. Forster is concerned, however, it seems not to have occurred to him that a generation might appear which would appreciate a more definite and detailed description of the novelist's method and we are left largely to hypothesis and inference.

Throughout the book there is abundant evidence of a desire on the part of Forster to monopolize Dickens as Watts-Dunton did Swinburne. The Dickens letters quoted are almost without exception addressed to Forster, although there is no reason to complain of a lack of letters. The point of view is that of an unflinching advocate prepared to defend the novelist not only against attack but even the possibility of mild criticism. Forster makes much of the letters which Dickens wrote him from America and particularly of the fact that he told in those letters much more than he later confided to the public in his "American Notes." Fortunately for us of today Forster was too blinded by affection to realize that the feeling which Dickens revealed was largely his own childish joy over the reception which those queer Americans gave him. It was his first taste of the sweets of fame and the fact that they were tendered him in cloying kind and quantity without much intelligence or discrimination did not affect the pleasure with which he received them. Aside from this, the information conveyed to Forster in his letters from America makes their exclusion from the "American Notes" of small importance.

It is impossible to avoid the conclusion that there should be another life of Dickens, not for the sake of refuting Forster so much as to do for him what Benson has done for Mrs. Gaskell, and incidentally to save Dickens from the smothering clutch of overrighteous affection. It is interesting, however, that in spite of a steady avoidance of even a mildly critical view of Dickens, the net result of the book is an emphasis of the naïve surprise and joy the novelist felt over his own success.

XII

THE BEGINNINGS OF THE NEW BIOGRAPHY

ANY attempt to discuss the biographical developments of the Victorian era is difficult and in large part futile because of certain unavoidable comparisons and overlapping tendencies and results. To discuss Carlyle, for example, as a student of biography in the light of the times in which he wrote or in respect to the aspect which he presented to the men of his time will leave that great figure without necessary illumination. It is particularly misleading to omit detailed treatment of "Thomas Carlyle" by James Anthony Froude, which did not appear until the Victorian era was so far advanced that it had largely ceased to be Victorian. Carlyle was in the modern sense no biographer, but a philosopher and moralist. It was the moral and philosophical aspects of his subjects which most attracted him and it was those phases which commanded the greater part of his attention.

134

In another sense, however, Carlyle was never anything but a biographer. Even his monumental "History of the French Revolution" was an extended and frequently hectic and incoherent treatment of individuals. To the modern student of that period the figures of Danton, Marat, and Robespierre are accidental and temporary flotsam that appears for a time on the crest of the flood presently to be rolled under. To Carlyle they were the dominating and to a large extent the creative masters of the whirlwind and then victims of its power. The social and economic forces that produced the Revolution present themselves to Carlyle's mind only in their philosophical aspects. The disaster which overwhelmed the old order was to him evidence of an avenging deity rather than of the irresistible working of economic and social processes.

By a curious reversal, his biography of Frederick the Great is in reality more a history than a biography, as his "History of the French Revolution" is more biography than history. This can be explained on the ground that since the beginning of his formal studies certain aspects of German literature and life had been to him of absorbing interest with the result that Frederick filled his eyes, first as a

German, and secondly as an outstanding
personality.

It must be admitted that "Frederick the
Great" is hard reading. In his "House Boat on
the Styx," John Kendrick Bangs pokes sly
humor at the ponderous pages. The shades of
Frederick, of Napoleon, of Shakespeare, Milton, and the rest are conversing idly in the
smoking room of the famous houseboat when
Shakespeare asks Frederick if he has ever read
his "Life" by Carlyle. To which Frederick
replies with a yawn that he has not yet found
time. Eternity was still too brief for such a
task.

In his "Life of Oliver Cromwell" Carlyle
stuck more closely to what had by that time
become the generally accepted method of
presentation, the use of letters, papers, diaries,
and other documentary material. It is on the
whole accurate and rather surprisingly free
from implications and conclusions, probably
because the Scotch philosopher found in the
hard-minded, practical soldier-administrator
little opportunity for either reasoning or rationalizing. To Cromwell the problems of this life
were comparatively simple and objective and
to be dealt with by musket and pike. The
problems of the future life he saw with al-

most equal clearness and simplicity. Such a man offers comparatively little opportunity for a writer of the Carlyle character and background.

The brief "Life of John Sterling" is probably the least read of any of Carlyle's writings, if in fact one can make such a distinction in the work of a man now largely relegated to a place of honor on library shelves. It was pre-eminently a work of love on Carlyle's part. Sterling, the moody, temperamental, finely organized young student and minister had won a close place in the Carlylean affections. The perfunctory and somewhat inaccurate sketch of Sterling by the Reverend Julius Hare, appearing soon after his death, aroused in Carlyle such a heat of indignation that he determined to set a picture of Sterling before the world. The result is to show, if not Sterling, at least Carlyle at his warmest if not his best.

But "Thomas Carlyle" by Froude is the necessary capstone for the Carlylean structure, or mausoleum if you please, although it was no cemetery adornment at the time of its publication. No better selection for a biographer of Carlyle could have been made than James Anthony Froude. He was closely acquainted with both the Carlyles, which met the Carlylean dictum that a biographer should have intimate personal knowledge of his subject. He was a trained historian, accustomed to the study and use of documents and the presentation of documentary material. He was not without experience in the writing of specialized biography as his "Life of Lord Beaconsfield" attests. He was well grounded in the Scotch school of philosophy which had produced Carlyle and he was intimately acquainted with the political activities of England which so occupied Carlyle's interests through his life. Not only did he have an intimate acquaintance with the Carlyles but he had access to most of the correspondence between Thomas and Jane.

In spite of his qualifications, however, Froude's "Life" aroused such a storm of criticism and denunciation as has seldom marked the publication of a book. He was denounced as a false friend, as an invader of secret intimacies, and as a violater of confidences entrusted to him by a man now beyond the possibility of explanation or defense. A reader of the Froude "Life" today will wonder more than a little at the storm that it produced. To begin with he had the warrant of the great man himself. Not only was the book written from material furnished by Carlyle, but according to an attitude requested by him: "The man as he was, growl and all."

In his review of Lockhart's "Life of Scott," Carlyle had vented his scorn on the conventional biography of his time and before: "How delicate, decent is English biography, bless its mealy mouth. A Damocles' sword of Respectability hangs forever over the poor English life-writer (as it does over poor English life in general) and reduces him to the verge of paralysis. Thus it has been said, 'There are no English lives worth reading, except those of players, who, by the nature of the case, have bidden respectability good day.'"

Those who venture into Froude's "Carlyle" today are likely to be somewhat amused to discover that one of the chief points of criticism is that the biographer revealed the unhappiness of the domestic relation. To be sure there was no scandal in the modern sense. Neither was there any public demonstration of unhappiness of the sort calculated to whet the appetite of the reader of the modern tabloid. Much of the fact which Froude presents and proves by letters was already known in general to the members of the Carlyle circle. It was no secret that Jane Welsh had been and remained a brilliant, high-spirited woman accustomed to a social environment and an ease of living which she was little likely to experience as the wife of Thomas Carlyle. To be sure, Froude revealed the existence of a love affair between Miss Welsh and Edward Irving, a brilliant, popular, eccentric preacher, later one of the most petted and courted figures of the dissenting persuasion in London.

After a long and uncertain courtship she elected to marry Carlyle and undertook to play the part of faithful wife to a dyspeptic, morose, only partially successful Scotch writer. At Craigenputtoch, where Carlyle soon after the marriage attempted to combine the functions of writer and farmer, she filled the role of household drudge, milking and making butter, killing and dressing poultry, scrubbing floors, washing clothes, doing all the varying and endless tasks of the Scotch housekeeper while Carlyle wrote and fumed and fretted and battered his head against all the stone walls that he could find.

His mother in his youth had said of him the first and last word: "Gey ill to live with."

Froude perhaps offers the key to Jane Welsh Carlyle's marriage with Thomas and her somewhat temperamental enduring of the hardships of life with him when he says: "But she was not happy. Long years after, in the late evening of her laborious life, she said: 'I married for ambition. Carlyle has exceeded all that my wildest hopes ever imagined of him—and I am miserable.'"

If this is an accurate quotation it is no wonder that Mr. Froude felt himself free to write of the Carlyle ménage as he did in the belief that in so doing he was doing more to present a faithful picture of Carlyle than by any process of selection or exclusion such as his critics declared he should have undertaken. Froude said of his own work that he might in truth have not produced a "Life" but only the material out of which a "Life" might some day be written. Even the modern critic must conclude that he has done more and better than that. In spite of the rather profuse quotation from letters, diaries, fragmentary writings, the result is Carlyle. To be sure, it is an earth-bound Carlyle, harassed by the daily details of the household, torturing himself by argument with editors and publishers who after the manner of their kind suggest

changes, demand condensations, deprecate
excesses of thought and of expression.

It was this experience that produced Carlyle.
To ignore his petty troubles is to fail to understand the man. Perhaps the best proof of
this would be to suggest the reading first of
the Froude "Carlyle" and then of Carlyle's
own "Sartor Resartus." If the result is not a
clearer understanding of both works, then
there is no likelihood of an understanding
of either. Carlyle and Froude should not be
dismissed without making it clear that the
much discussed "Life" is not merely a collection of annotated letters or a presentation
of a series of documentary tempests in a
half-literary, half-philosophical teapot. Froude
knew the Scotch, he knew his Carlyles, and
in spite of his hard, practical, historical mind
he knew the tragedy of life. This knowledge
now and again spurred him to something like
eloquence, as in the passage in which he
pictures the Carlyle family fading away into
the mists:

"Margaret Carlyle sleeps in Ecclefechan
churchyard. Her father followed soon and
was laid beside her. Then after him, but not
for many years, the pious, tender, original,
beautiful-minded mother. John Carlyle was

the next of their children who rejoined them, and next he of whom I am writing. The world and the world's business scatter families to the four winds, but they collect again in death. Alick lies far off in a Canadian resting place; but in his last illness, when the memory wanders, he too had traveled in spirit back to Annandale and the old days when his brother was at college, and with the films of the last struggle closing over his eyes he asked anxiously if 'Tom was come back from Edinburgh.'"

The moral earnestness of which Mr. Strachey complains brought a considerable number of biographies and autobiographies into existence in the last century, and some of these could not well be spared, at least by the student of literature or of thought. Two of these that stand out above the others are John Stuart Mill's "Autobiography" and "Apologia pro vita sua" by Cardinal Newman. To even the student of today Mill is a bloodless, remote, merciless analyst of the economic and philosophical relations of men. He was the intellectual leader of the classical economists of his day and a master of the power of abstract thought with few peers in England or any other country, then or ever. His "Essay on Liberty" was a close analysis and a clear statement of the principles and historical bases of human liberty that marked a long advance beyond the turgid thinking and bombastic writing to which the French Revolution had given birth. His economic theories have long since fallen into disrepute, although an American senator only a month before this paragraph was written announced that nothing had happened to change or to supplant the political economy of John Stuart Mill. The senator is doubtless happy though lonesome in this belief.

Whether justly or not, little remains of Mill but a shadow. His "Autobiography" gives the shadow substance if not life. Probably the most interesting passages are those describing his education. In fact, it is those passages which give the key to the purpose of the entire book. Mill was a product of an educational experiment. His father, James Mill, was a severe and destructive critic of the English school system and set himself to the training of his son as an example of what should be done. Judging from the result, the young John Stuart was nothing short of a prodigy or the method was nothing short of a miracle. He began the study of Latin at the age of eight, but by way of making it clear that his youth was not entirely wasted, he explains that by that time he had read Herodotus, Xenophon's "Cyropaedia" and "Memorials of Socrates," some of Diogenes Laertius's "Lives of Philosophers," part of Lucian, and Isocrates' "Ad Demonicum" and "Ad Nicoclem." He also admits to having read the first six dialogues of Plato, naïvely confessing that the sixth might well have been omitted, "as it was totally impossible that I should understand it."

The man into whom this youthful wonder grew justified his father's hopes, at least so far as his power to comprehend, analyze, and express the intellectual movements of his time was concerned.

Cardinal Newman's autobiography is a personal narrative and a documentation of one of the serious and engrossing periods in the history of English philosophical and religious thought. It is easy to dismiss the Oxford movement as a struggle between high church and low and then as a struggle between Catholic and Anglican or to find in it little more than formal and formalistic discussions of ritual and tradition. Probably an Oxford movement could not occur again, certainly not today. On the other hand, if it occurred it would almost certainly not partake of those characteristics of formalism that we moderns so easily and mistakenly ascribe to the movement of nearly a century ago. Modern physics and biology had not yet appeared to rewrite man's conception of the universe and his place in it, or to so widen the physical boundaries of the universe and alter our conception of the forces that move within it; men still felt under the necessity of determining their view of these matters by the sheer power of abstract thinking. It was this quality underlying the formalistic traditional conventional disputes that gave the Oxford movement a character and an importance.

Newman was both a force and a result in the movement, a force not only because of his intellectual ability but because of his sincere, unflagging, spiritual energy. If the reading of his "Apologia" is followed by the chapter on Manning in Strachey's "Eminent Victorians," an admirably balanced result will be secured. The fact is that they belong together not so much as correctives as in a curious way supplementary. It was not within the power of the great cardinal to make of himself either a hero or a martyr. It certainly was not the intent of Strachey to do so either. In fact the reader senses between the lines of Strachey a kind of wonder that any man could be such a fool and in the end may conclude in spite of Strachey that the folly was touched with divine courage.

Perhaps Newman's writings were the last great assertion of the old principle of complete resignation to the divine will, as Theodore Parker's were the first broad statement of the modern thesis of the will of the individual. If that is true, "Apologia pro vita sua" marks the end of a great epoch.

XIII

MACAULAY

An exception to the rule of the dangerous effect of kinship on biography is Sir George Otto Trevelyan's "Life and Letters of Lord Macaulay." In spite of the fact that he was a nephew of the man about whom he wrote and closer to his uncle than is sometimes the lot of nephews, Sir George wrote a competent, readable, and almost a great biography. What remains to us is an intimate, clear, well-written account of a full and more than ordinarily interesting life. Naturally, it was not possible for the author of the "History of the American Revolution" to write other than well and accurately. Neither was it possible for a nephew of Lord Macaulay, a sharer in the great Whig tradition, an intimate and at times almost daily companion of that cramped but fascinating personality, to fail to be charmed and to communicate the charm to his own readers.

Of all the writers in the later years of Victoria's reign, Lord Macaulay was prob-

ably the most industrious, the most varied
in his interests and certainly the most productive in results. As Thackeray said of him,
he would search for a week to correct a date
and travel a hundred miles to verify an impression. Probably this attitude of mind was more
remarkable in the rather easy-going school
of historical research in which Macaulay was
bred than in our own day. The painstaking
care with which Macaulay worked on his
narrative passages is illustrated by Trevelyan
with extracts from his diary covering the
days in which he was writing the story of
Glencoe, a stirring but not important episode
in history.

"That author must have had a strong head,
and no very exaggerated self-esteem, who
while fresh from a literary success which had
probably never been equalled, and certainly
never surpassed—at a time when the book-
sellers were waiting with almost feverish
eagerness for anything that he chose to give
them—spent nineteen working days over
thirty octavo pages, and ended by humbly
acknowledging that the result was not to his
mind."

To the readers of today the Macaulay style
seems marked with a kind of metallic lucidity

rather than with the suggestive charm more
to the taste of the moderns. But the passing
of Macaulay from the historical and literary
stage should not turn away the student of
literature and particularly of biography from
the Trevelyan life. The boy who boasted to
his schoolfellows that his uncle had written a
history of England in two volumes and that
there were six hundred and fifty pages in each
volume lived to erect a monument to that
uncle's memory which deserves to be read
for its own sake.

That all great lives are not matter for
great biography is rather clearly indicated
in Alexander V. G. Allen's "Phillips Brooks."
Phillips Brooks was the great American divine
in the latter half of the last century. Throughout his ministry in Trinity Church in Boston,
crowds flocked to hear him as to a theatrical
spectacle. But what they saw and heard
was more than this. Brooks was a rare soul
combining intellectual power, spiritual fervor,
wide understanding, and tolerance, with
great physical charm, almost beauty. A
stranger at one of his services said at the
close: "I feel as if the Gods had come down
again to earth."

At the beginning of his ministry, the officers of the church were overwhelmed with this inrush of strangers. Many doubted the value of preaching that could so compel attention and one good bishop betook himself to another place of worship, where he might meditate in quiet, free from the oppression of other worshipers and the disturbing influence that seemed to radiate from the pulpit. In many minds the question arose, "Can a man be popular and orthodox?"—although throughout his long activity no basis for seriously questioning the orthodoxy of Phillips Brooks seemed to present itself.

But Allen's life of the great divine presents only a shadow of his greatness. It echoes faintly in the extracts from sermons, it peers out occasionally in his letters, it shows dimly in occasional mild anecdotes of his humanness, his charm, his humor. The man himself remains behind a veil. It is Brooks who gives the key to this apparent mystery. Himself a sedulous reader of biography, he remarked on one occasion that he would rather have written a great biography than any other kind of a great book. He admitted that there were men who, because of the nature of their work, were unsuited for biographical treatment. Such men, according to Brooks, were Shakespeare, Shelley, and Wordsworth. "The lives of these men are in their poetry."

Phillips Brooks's life was in his sermons. And a commentary on the sermons preached through an active ministry of thirty years, however great they may have been, however stirring and vital their appeal may have been to congregations, is not biography. Probably it is the fate of Phillips Brooks, great as he was during his life, to remain to us only an echo, growing fainter with the years.

XIV

LINCOLN—ANOTHER MYSTERY

THERE is one man in the American gallery
about whose biographies it is not easy to
write. That man is Abraham Lincoln. There
is a temptation to say of Lincoln that no one
suffered more during his lifetime from the
attacks of his enemies and no one has suffered
more since his death from the praise of his
friends. The glorification and to some extent
the obscuring of Lincoln began before the grass
was green over his grave. William Herndon,
his old law partner at Springfield, was one
of the earliest but probably not the worst of
the offenders. Herndon's book, now out of
print, was at least honest. Angered by the
deification of the man he knew so intimately
and admired so warmly, he attempted the
thankless task of presenting a human Lincoln,
the awkward country lawyer who sprawled
across a table or a bed in a tavern, or tilted
back in a chair with his feet elevated to the
mantle top; who told rude, sometimes obscene,
stories but always stories with a point of

wit or of wisdom; who dominated every group in which he found himself by the power of his personality, but who was certainly not a god and not even god-inspired according to Herndon. The worshipers of Lincoln were in no mood for such a treatment and Herndon's "Life of Lincoln" evoked a storm of criticism. Few of the critics however have produced better books about their hero.

The next important chapter in the Lincoln story was a long one written by John G. Nicolay and John Hay, his secretaries, "Abraham Lincoln, A History." What these two men did, Nicolay, the careful, meticulous, crabbed bureaucrat, and Hay, the gay, brilliant, mercurial man of letters, is a mixture of history and biography, too long for any one's careful reading, too diffuse to present a clear picture of the man whom they both by turns ridiculed and worshiped, too all-inclusive to be inscribed accurately even as the "life and times" of Lincoln. But it is and will remain an admirable source book for the student who wishes to study Lincoln and the collateral happenings of the Lincoln time at near and reliable second-hand. The abridged edition written by Nicolay and Hay is only an abridgment.

It was not until more than thirty years after Lincoln died that a really good, concise life of the war president appeared. This was "The Life of Abraham Lincoln" by Ida M. Tarbell, a thoroughly trained student of history, a journalist, and a remarkable observer. Beginning merely as an attempt to collect personal recollections of Lincoln from men who had known him and had worked with him in some phase of his tragic odyssey, the history developed naturally and easily. It has the merits of crispness of outline, definiteness of plan, regularity of progression, and thorough unity of composition. Little that has been discovered since its writing adds to the necessary information or detracts from the value of what Miss Tarbell did.

Perhaps if one were to attempt to list the lives of Lincoln that have in our time contributed something to the saga, there would be danger of historical or critical injustice. Would the thoroughly scholarly and sound "Abraham Lincoln" by John T. Morse, Jr., in the American Statesmen Series, appear in such a list? It is to be doubted. And yet the reader who knows only Morse still knows most of that which is essential to an understanding of Lincoln, barring one thing, which is a realization that a man born in the backwoods is inevitably a backwoodsman and that that fact is neither a virtue nor a vice but a natural consequence and offers no cause for wonder, for censure, or for praise.

Carl Sandburg's "Abraham Lincoln, The Prairie Years" is only in part a life of Lincoln. Perhaps it might more properly be labeled a prose poem of prairie life which gave birth to this immortal figure. The drama is complete even to the blowing of the wind through the prairie grasses, the murmur of the Sangamon, and the nodding of the flowers on Ann Rutledge's grave. But the Lincoln that emerges is somewhat sentimentalized, as the Lincoln of Herndon was somewhat gross.

Dr. William E. Barton added many details to the Lincoln record, many of them important at least in rounding out the picture and in settling minor controversies that had created debate out of comparison to their importance. Some of his discoveries, however, are in matters that might well have been ignored, such as, for example, the question of Lincoln's legitimacy. There is also the manner and time of the writing of the Gettysburg address, although on this point Dr. Barton elects to be mildly humorous in his delving in the historical scrap heap. It is easy to agree with Dr. Barton's implied conclusion that it is of little importance whether the Gettysburg address was written in Washington the day before the ceremony or on the train from Washington to Gettysburg or in the hotel the night before or half an hour before the meeting began. The fact is that it was written in the mind and character of the man in all the years of his life up to that point.

Senator Beveridge's "Abraham Lincoln" is the work of a lawyer, satisfactory if one finds satisfaction in a lawyer's brief, but not by any means the last word to those who believe that the story of a man's life lies somewhere outside the written record, sometimes outside the field of evidence entirely. Incidentally Mr. Beveridge repeats many of the statements made by Herndon and proves them from the record. Yet Beveridge is praised and Herndon is condemned.

Lord Charnwood contributed a graceful scholarly English estimate in "Abraham Lincoln"—just, true, but still English. Can an Englishman understand an American three thousand miles away and seventy years in the past? Can an American understand him? Perhaps there is no answer. Doubtless, though,

no life of Lincoln has yet been written superior
to the Charnwood book as literary portraiture.

Read any or all of these and then read the
autobiography which Lincoln wrote at the
request of Jesse W. Fell in 1859 and take
your choice.

"I was born February 12, 1809, in Hardin
County, Kentucky. My parents were both
born in Virginia, of undistinguished families—
second families, perhaps I should say. My
mother, who died in my tenth year, was of a
family of the name of Hanks, some of whom
now reside in Adams, and others in Macon
County, Illinois. My paternal grandfather,
Abraham Lincoln, emigrated from Rocking-
ham County, Virginia, to Kentucky about
1781 or 1782, where a year or two later he
was killed by the Indians, not in battle, but
by stealth, when he was laboring to open a
farm in the forest. His ancestors, who were
Quakers, went to Virginia from Berks County,
Pennsylvania. An effort to identify them
with the New England family of the same
name ended in nothing more definite than a
similarity of Christian names in both families,
such as Enoch, Levi, Mordecai, Solomon,
Abraham, and the like.

"My father, at the death of his father, was
but six years of age, and he grew up literally

without education. He removed from Kentucky to what is now Spencer County, Indiana, in my eighth year. We reached our new home about the time the State came into the Union. It was a wild region, with many bears and other wild animals still in the woods. There I grew up. There were some schools, so called, but no qualification was ever required of a teacher beyond readin', writin', and cipherin' to the rule of three. If a straggler supposed to understand Latin happened to sojourn in the neighborhood, he was looked upon as a wizard. There was absolutely nothing to excite ambition for education. Of course, when I came of age I did not know much. Still, somehow, I could read, write, and cipher to the rule of three, but that was all. I have not been to school since. The little advance I now have upon this store of education, I have picked up from time to time under the pressure of necessity.

"I was raised to farm work, which I continued till I was twenty-two. At twenty-one I came to Illinois, Macon County. Then I got to New Salem, at that time in Sangamon, now in Menard County, where I remained a year as a sort of clerk in a store. Then came the Black Hawk war; and I was elected a captain of volunteers, a success which gave me more pleasure than any I have had since. I went the campaign, was elated, ran for the legislature the same year (1832), and was beaten—the only time I ever have been beaten by the people. The next and three succeeding biennial elections I was elected to the legislature. I was not a candidate afterward. During this legislative period I had studied law, and removed to Springfield to practice it.

"In 1846 I was once elected to the lower House of Congress. Was not a candidate for reelection. From 1849 to 1854, both inclusive, practised law more assiduously than ever before. Always a Whig in politics; and generally on the Whig electoral tickets, making active canvasses. I was losing interest in politics when the repeal of the Missouri compromise aroused me again. What I have done since then is pretty well known.

"If any personal description of me is thought desirable, it may be said I am, in height, six feet four inches, nearly; lean in flesh, weighing on an average one hundred and eighty pounds; dark complexion, with coarse black hair and gray eyes. No other marks or brands recollected."

XV

NINETEENTH CENTURY AUTOBIOGRAPHY

THE nineteenth century, particularly its latter half, was especially productive of genuine life stories in the form of memoirs, autobiographies, and recollections. Many, if not most, of these are of slight importance for the general student of the current of life writing. Here and there, however, appears a man so important in his time and in the record which he left that the story of his life becomes a milestone for the students of human thought. Such a verdict can be rendered, for example, in the case of Thomas Huxley's autobiography. Huxley was something more than a scientist. In interests and attainments he was versatile, human, searching, and discriminating. His personal contacts were many, his domestic life warm and rich, and his points of contact with life itself extraordinarily varied for a man of so definite a field of specialized industry. All of these qualities bear fruit by implication in his "Autobiography," which should be read in connection with his "Selected Essays."

In addition, he was the great protagonist of evolution at a time when the evolutionary hypothesis propounded by Wallace, Darwin, and himself was an issue that threatened to cleave the church, if not society itself. In Huxley's resourceful, keen, and clever tongue the scientific group found an able ally and interpreter, as Bishop Wilberforce learned to his cost on one historic occasion. The good bishop had rashly referred to Huxley's apparent preference for a tree-dwelling ancestry. Huxley's counter was swift and hard in his comment on the bishop's preference for a selected ancestry rather than for the truth.

Not all of the scientists are so happy in their autobiographical efforts. To Darwin his own life was largely a hard, sometimes fruitless, wholly absorbing search for scientific evidence in the field of his study. This search largely blotted out from his vision the lighter, simpler things of life which to Huxley remained so interesting to the end. It is in his "Autobiographical Chapter" in the "Life and Letters" edited by his son that Darwin vaguely laments the fact that in his later years he had been able to discover in himself no taste for the theater, for music, or for literature, except the hard literature of his own subject.

Herbert Spencer can hardly be said to have written an autobiography at all in "An Autobiography," but rather a continuation of his synthetic philosophy. To be sure the reader with a sense of humor may find matter for a smile here and there but that reader may be sure that the smile was not of the philosopher's intention. A faint example is his disgusted experiment with deep breathing as a cure for insomnia, his shattered, sensitive nerves reacting in exactly the wrong direction. His contempt for the majority of mankind is expressed in his account of his appearance in the parlor of his lodging house with his ears covered tight by a pair of old-fashioned ear muffs in order that he might not be annoyed by the conversation of the other lodgers.

Both Darwin and Spencer, each in his own way, has written the record of his life as he saw it, reflecting those things which each found interesting. But neither contributed materially to the literary color of the growing biographical stream and neither offers much to illuminate life today.

It is in this latter half of the century that America makes a real contribution that probably can never be ignored, "The Memoirs of General U. S. Grant." The "Memoirs" themselves could probably be dismissed in a few words without injustice. They are as plain and blunt, as lacking in artifice, as the man himself and to that extent are competent autobiography. Every page bears evidence that this is the work of no ghost writer but of a soldier more at home in the saddle than at the desk. It was written near the end of his life when the shadows were closing in. The concluding chapters were penned in the full knowledge that death was near. No indication of this, however, occurs in the text itself and the last pages are as simple, as matter of fact, and as workmanlike as the beginning.

It is for the understanding of Grant that echoes through these pages that the biographical student of today should read the "Memoirs." No national hero ever shone more brilliantly than did Grant at the end of the Civil War and probably no other ever subjected himself afterward, as though deliberately, to experiences and performances calculated to dim his own luster. Many times his friends must have wished that his eight years in the presidency and the tragic experience of his financial adventure in New York City might be blotted from men's memories. And that wish has come near to realization. The Grant that remains with us is the Grant of the Civil War, not the President, and certainly not the financier.

There was in him something elemental, primitive, appealing, so that in the memory of old men so long as direct memories of the Civil War endured his name was like a drum beat, resounding, thrilling, commanding.

The "Memoirs" are worth reading for another reason. Their pages are ample evidence that here was no great tactician, no student of war, no lover even of the shock of action, as were Lee and Sherman. Early in the book, in recounting his experiences in the Mexican campaign, he admits somewhat shamefacedly to the capture of a wounded Mexican colonel and compares himself to the man who had boasted to his commander that he had cut off the leg of an enemy. When he was asked why he had not cut off the head instead, the hero replied: "Someone had done that before."

Grant saw in war no glory, no chance for self-aggrandizement, no waving banners, but

a dirty job that needed doing. Fort Henry,
Fort Donaldson, Vicksburg, The Wilderness,
Petersburg, Appomattox, all the way he was
the hard, dour, unexcited workman doing a
job and the job is there in his "Memoirs,"
written as life was ending. Whatever may
happen to the American people in the future,
so long as this volume remains in second-
hand bookstalls and on dusty library shelves
there will be available a picture of a native
American bred of the soil and never free from
the taint of it and the vernacular of the people
among whom he was born.

A strange figure in the literary museum
is that presented by Phineas Taylor Barnum
in his "Autobiography." Every man and
most women past fifty, the age which permits
them to have been young in the eighties, somewhere in America, remembers Barnum. He
was the showman par excellence, the father
of press-agentry in the world of American
entertainment. He may not have been the
author of that immortal phrase: "There's a
sucker born every minute," but no one knew
its truth so well as P. T. Barnum.

His career as a showman began with Joice
Heth, the negro woman of unbelievable age.

One hundred and twenty-five was the figure finally arrived at as sufficiently large to be impressive and not so large as to be entirely unbelievable. It was Joice Heth for whom was created, partly by Barnum and partly by others, that impressive fairy tale which involved the infant George Washington to whom she was reported on excellent evidence to have been nurse. The excellence of the evidence can not be doubted. It was manufactured by men born to that sort of literary effort and trained in the technique of it by long practice.

Barnum was the discoverer and exploiter of General Tom Thumb. He made Jumbo the greatest of all elephants; he was the sponsor for the white rhinoceros, the sacred white elephant of Siam, Chang, the Chinese giant, the wild man from Borneo, and other classics of our youth known throughout America. He even toured Europe with these and kindred attractions, had the privilege of presenting General Tom Thumb to Queen Victoria, and thereby added still further stars to his press-agent's crown.

That he should have written his "Autobiography" is not to be wondered at. Many such men have sought immortality by that road. The wonder is that Barnum achieved not literature but possibly something better—reality. Every page of this old book is alive with anecdotes, with self-revelation, with moralizing, with gleeful accounts of triumphs, with woeful confessions of unexpected failure. If he has illusions about himself they do not hamper his self-revealing. To a world still professing a firm belief in frugality, industry, and persistence as cardinal virtues he confesses: "I never really liked to work."

On one page he may tell the tale of a species of fraud so blatant for all its humor as to be almost actionable and on the next he professes his constant and consistent morality and his continued adherence to the precepts and practices of the Christian religion. The man who appears throughout these pages is the Yankee trader—shrewd, slippery, unscrupulous when necessary, resourceful always, rejoicing in a good trade, swallowing a bad one as merely another score that he proposes to even up at the first opportunity, intent on the main chance but thrilled with a hazardous gamble along the road to fortune. It was his fate to deal in a commodity the nature of which causes it to fade except as a thrilling or amusing memory as soon as the "big top" is struck and the wagons are on their way to the next town. There is therefore no reason to expect a literary resurrection for Barnum and perhaps he is the more fortunate thereby.

But this battered old book still to be found here and there in libraries or occasionally on secondhand bookstalls is a breath of reality blowing through the rather stuffy, self-conscious, highly stilted literary drawing rooms of America in the last century.

Autobiography is of all sorts, from Cellini to Henry Adams. Autobiographical writing varies in its subject matter and its objectives as widely as human interests and purposes vary. Probably comparatively few lives contain throughout their length genuinely important subject matter. Even an autobiography of Washington might contain dry stretches, particularly his version of his struggles to bring his Mount Vernon farm back to prosperous cultivation.

As a result, the examination of most autobiographies is likely to show many chapters not essentially autobiographical but historical, critical, or narrative, containing autobiography only in the indirect reflection of the writer. Now and again, however, a writer

appears with a story pertaining to a limited
period of his life that is of intense interest,
not because of outward events but because of
inward growth and struggles. One outstanding
result of such a process is Edmund William
Gosse's "Father and Son." This book was
published in 1907, but the period with which
it deals is the childhood and youth of the
writer in the middle of the last century. This
was the time of savage and what threatened
to be mortal combat between the forces of
orthodox religion and the new and growing
friends of science.

This struggle was intensified in a narrow
and for a time almost tragic manner in the
relationship of Edmund Gosse with his father
and mother. In the profession and attitude
of the father, the two elements warred. By
profession he was a scientist, although not
of a creative or particularly productive kind.
Thomas Huxley called him "an honest hod-
man of science." His scientific work apparently
had no relation to his religious life which went
on as though in a separate airtight and idea-
tight compartment. He and his wife were
members of the small strict sect of Plymouth
Brethren. The Plymouth Brethren were literal-
ists in regard to the Scripture and probably

represented the last survival of Calvinistic Puritanism in England. Their meetings, held for many years in the Gosse home, were, as described by Gosse, strongly reminiscent of the early Puritan gatherings. There was no ritual, there was no order of service, the foundation of their worship was a reading and a literal exposition of the Scripture accompanied by the singing of doleful hymns, long prayers, and sermons calculated to reach and impress the minds of the peasants and laborers who constituted the greater part of the congregation.

One marked characteristic was the strongly anti-Catholic bias. Even Christmas was denounced as popish and heathenish. On one occasion, a maid in the household gave to six-year-old Edmund a slice of the forbidden Christmas pudding. The immediate result was a violent stomach-ache and a small boy running in terror of his immortal soul to his father crying: "Oh papa, papa, I have eaten of flesh offered to idols."

A considerable part of the body of the book deals with the experiences of the father as head of a group of the Brethren on the Devon coast, but interwoven is the thread of the son's growing unrest, unsatisfied curiosity, and

increasing efforts to break the bonds by which
he felt himself held. At one place he speaks
of his own consciousness as growing "in a
huddled mixture of Endymion and the Book
of Revelation, John Wesley's hymns and
Midsummer Night's Dream."

As a picture of child psychology, "Father
and Son" is a complete document. The small
boy, brought up in an atmosphere of literal
belief and wholehearted acceptance, prayed
for a humming top that he had seen in a shop
window, adding the customary protective
formula, "If it is thy will." No top was
forthcoming and the father remonstrated
with the boy, telling him that he should not
pray for "things like that." Naturally the
boy asked why.

"And I added that he said we ought to
pray for things we needed, and that I needed
the humming top a great deal more than I
did the conversion of the heathen or the
restitution of Jerusalem to the Jews, two
objects of my nightly supplication which
left me very cold. . . . The fatal suspicion had crossed my mind that the reason
why I was not to pray for the top was because it was too expensive for my parents
to buy. . . . "

At about this time the boy was whipped for some childish act and in his anger decided to commit an act of idolatry, praying to a chair and waiting for the disaster that he had expected would come upon him. No disaster appeared and further ammunition was added to the boy's stock of doubt as to the sufficiency and reality of his father's faith.

Sometime later, at the age of ten or thereabouts, the boy sought permission to accept an invitation to a children's party near by. The father's austere soul rebelled at such a sinful and worldly pastime and finally compromised on a prayer for light. At the conclusion of the prayer, the father turned to young Edmund with an expression of relief and an air of hearty congratulation that another knotty problem had been solved and inquired: "Well, and what is the answer which our Lord vouchsafes?" Here was the occasion for Edmund's first outward rebellion. He replied in the high piping accents of despair: "The Lord says I may go to the Browns." And he went.

Nowhere outside of the formal chronicles and discussions of this scientific-religious controversy, which was shaking the English world, is there to be found a more illuminating account of the smaller but then vital aspects of the battle. It is amusing now to read of the book which the elder Gosse wrote in which he proposed to reconcile forever the conflicting claims of science and religion. At that time the chief stumbling block was the difficulty of reconciling the chronology and history of the first chapter of Genesis with that written in the geological strata, but it was not difficult to the elder Gosse. His book referred to creation as the literal act of six literal days, following which practically no change had taken place in the surface of the earth. The apparent indications of earlier forms of life and an immensely greater age were included in the original construction by the creator in order, as the elder Gosse naïvely suggested, to arouse the curiosity of his children, or perhaps to test their wavering faith.

To his astonishment and horror the book was rejected by both parties with almost equal scorn. Charles Kingsley, his friend and confidant, on whose understanding and support he had counted with confidence, denounced it as an attempt to prove that "God had written on the rocks one enormous and superfluous lie."

"Father and Son" is not only documentary. It is literature, a result not surprising, of course, from the author of the lives of Swinburne, Congreve, Gray, Donne, Jeremy Taylor, Sir Thomas Browne, and of all the volumes of essays, criticisms, and even verse that poured from the pen of Edmund Gosse. It was no apprentice pen that wrote of his father's prayers: "It might be said that he stormed the citadels of God's grace, refusing to be baffled, urging his intercessions without mercy upon a Deity who sometimes struck me as inattentive to his prayers or wearied by them."

If more autobiographies were written in the spirit of this, from a desire to present to the readers those aspects and experiences of life that are of fundamental and lasting importance in the shaping of personality, there would be fewer autobiographies written and perhaps better ones. But the writing of autobiography would become a more difficult art.

When "The Education of Henry Adams," by Henry Adams, appeared in 1918, having been privately printed in 1906, a mild controversy began which has not entirely disappeared. Opinion was divided. To some it was the dreary moan of a misanthrope who sought from life a special satisfaction which life can not and should not offer. To others it seemed more the measured, calculated sneer of a super-developed New England intellect which felt itself superior to a world which was not designed to recognize its superiority. The unprejudiced reader, coming to this book free from the discussions that its first appearance evoked, may fairly reach a conclusion quite different from either of these. In fact, it is the conclusion which is repeatedly indicated by the author and in many cases emphasized and strongly insisted upon. It is the education of Henry Adams and nothing more. To put it more bluntly, it is the struggle of Henry Adams for an education.

To understand it, it is not necessary to characterize either the book or the author as misanthropic or cynical or superior. The proof that the writer felt anything but superior throughout a considerable part of his life is to be found on every page. That he thought himself a failure is equally demonstrated and at the end of his life in 1910 he had decided to leave it in manuscript, unpublished by choice, except for the private printing four years earlier. That it was published is due to the Massachusetts Historical Society.

The education that Henry Adams sought was an understanding of the world and his place in it, not an unreasonable quest, although probably one beyond hope of realization. The distinctive quality in Adams and in his autobiography is the fact that he refused to be satisfied with half truth, with partial answers, with seeming explanations. Conventional processes did not satisfy him. As he looked back at his undergraduate days at Harvard, he wrote: "The four years passed at college were, for his purposes, wasted. Harvard College was a good school, but at bottom what the boy disliked most was any school at all. He did not want to be one in a hundred—one per cent of an education. He regarded himself as the only person for whom his education had value, and he wanted the whole of it. He got barely half of an average."

There is a singular resemblance in this point to a similar comment of Gibbon as he looked back, from almost the same point in his life, at his fourteen months in Magdalen.

There is another point of comparison with the historian of Rome. Adams sat, like Gibbon, on Ara Coeli and like Gibbon listened to the chanting of the Franciscan friars. But here the resemblance ends. No inspiration and no determination came to Adams. The fall of Rome remained as inexplicable, as unreasonable, as baffling as ever.

Men puzzled Adams. It was his fortune to be in Palermo when Garibaldi's ten thousand were mustered for the advance on Rome and to call upon Garibaldi with official dispatches. Being Henry Adams, he looked back forty years after to see what remained in his mind of Garibaldi and to discover, if possible, an explanation of the mystery of life. What he saw was this: "The lesson of Garibaldi, as education, seemed to teach the extreme complexity of extreme simplicity; but one could have learned this from a glow-worm. One did not need the vivid recollection of the low-voiced, simple-mannered seafaring captain, of Genoese adventurers and Sicilian brigands, supping in the July heat and Sicilian dirt and revolutionary clamor, among the barricaded streets of insurgent Palermo, merely in order to remember that simplicity is complex."

Within a year he was in Washington and saw the new President, Abraham Lincoln. "He saw a long, awkward figure; a plain, ploughed face; a mind, absent in part, and in part evidently worried by white kid gloves; features that expressed neither self-satisfaction nor any other familiar Americanism, but rather the same painful sense of becoming educated and of needing education that tormented a private secretary; above all a lack of apparent force."

During the first administration of Grant he was in Washington as observer and journalist. He found plenty of material for his pen in the episodes and the scandals that characterized the administration. But Grant as a symbol of progress, as a proof of the advance of evolution, puzzled him even more than Garibaldi or Lincoln. "Garibaldi seemed to him a trifle the more intellectual, but, in both, the intellect counted for nothing; only the energy counted."

If this torpid, slow-moving, slow-thinking mysterious man in the White House was the result of evolution, then Adams could conclude only that evolution was ridiculous.

The "Education of Henry Adams" is not for the light or the careless reader. Least of all is it for those bright spirits who believe that if this is not the best of all possible worlds, it is soon to become so. Perhaps the book might be recommended as a warning of the danger of indulging in the intellectual life, for it was intellect that tortured Adams throughout his life. He saw too much, too far, too broadly ever to make up his mind. Where less intellectual critics reached conclusions and then excluded contrary evidence, Adams continued to find conflicting phenomena, continued to be puzzled, finally concluding that there was no answer to the questions which life asked of him and which he impertinently asked of life.

He did, however, reach certain conclusions, the conclusions of a philosopher rather than of a journalist. As he searches back through his life and projects that life back into the Middle Ages, he grows less and less certain of the power of intellect in the world. Neither can he find satisfactory evidence of consistent progress. Thought is a result and not a cause. Discoveries and inventions are a gift of nature plus a not especially high order of observation, and he cites Newton and the apple, Watt and the steam engine, Franklin and the kite. "Certain men merely held out their hands and great forces of nature stuck to them, as though they were playing ball."

Two things he deduced and there the book ends. One is a dynamic theory of history; that not progress, not improvement, not even retrogradation is the lesson of two thousand years, but solely the gathering and growing value and significance of force, of energy. The chief contribution of Christianity, concludes Adams, has been in the elevation of the cross through the Middle Ages as a new symbol of force. The two discoveries or inventions which effectually broke the shackles of medievalism, the compass and gunpowder, have been useful not as making the world better or worse, but as manifestations of force, and their contributions have been in that realm for the most part blind, unknowing, and uncaring.

And his second conclusion is that there is a law of acceleration of force. In this phrase he explains the nineteenth century and offers such light as he may for the twentieth. For in this process of change and of motion which Adams finds in the world as a result of this development and acceleration of force, again he finds little conscious intelligence or deliberate intent. Individuals here and there have held out their hands and nature has dropped in them apples or kite strings or a bit of magnetized iron or a handful of chemicals. Individuals organized in government or in society and religious bodies have contributed less than nothing either to individual changes or to the process of change. He sees that the customary attitude of organized society in whatever form is one of opposition to any change.

And there is the "Education of Henry Adams," the only book of its kind in existence, perhaps the only book of its kind that should be written, but it can not be dismissed lightly or in anger. Whether a milestone in human thinking or a solitary stone dropped at the end of a long road, it is one of the biographical contributions of the early twentieth century, a book that probably could not have been written at an earlier time and one that certainly would not have been published then.

XVI

THE MODERNS

THE moderns in biography are as difficult to define as in other forms of art. The critic soon learns to distrust all easy distinctions, especially those of an epigrammatic character. Differences are seldom so obvious, nor do they so easily exist for the purposes of the clever builder of phrases. Subtle and involved classifications are equally dangerous. They are hard to understand, and when understood, hard to apply.

Biographers are prone today to make much use of the word "psychology." Is it the true mark of the modern? Francis Hackett calls his "Henry VIII" a "psychic biography." We must absolve Mr. Hackett of any irregularity as to the sources of his material. There is no crystal gazing or automatic writing in his book. It is carefully documented, although we may be permitted to lift a questioning eyebrow at his statement that there is not a line or phrase of dialogue for which he cannot cite chapter and verse. Copious as are the Tudor records, are they really as thorough as he implies?

But that word "psychic." Does Mr. Hackett mean that here is something new? And what is it? I seem to recall that Plutarch was concerned about the soul of man—that mysterious quality that gives color, individuality to life. Is he seeking to look behind the curtain that hides personality? Surely no one sought more earnestly to pierce the unknown than did St. Augustine. Or does he mean merely that he will show us man—a man—as he is? Can he rival the brutal frankness of Cellini?

Perhaps we are on safer ground if we agree that the moderns are the moderns, the men and women of our own time. Certainly a book written in the last twenty years has been born out of the environment of which we are a part. But for purposes of critical analysis "modern" should mean something more lasting than "now." What will the biographies of our time be called in a hundred years, when new moderns look down the century at such books as remain on earth? I do not know which they will be, but some will still be found—if only as literary curiosities—and the question of what to call them may then be answered.

In the meantime, not as a prophecy, but as a modest suggestion to posterity, one reader of biography may record his belief that the prime difference of the new from the old biographies is religious and philosophical and not intellectual. In the mind of the older writer there was little conscious doubt that this life is a pilgrimage to a better world, a place of trial and temptation, the supreme issues of which would be determined elsewhere. If this life is merely an antechamber to eternity—and especially if there is a rather definite theory about eternity—then the visible lives of men must be judged according to that theory. In the light of that belief good and bad became quite definite qualities. Here and there men might still recall Socrates's definition of virtue, but as a rule the safer plan to follow was that of assuming that goodness was best acquired by following an external and accepted pattern. Such goodness was easily recognized and recorded.

This is not the place to discuss changes in religious belief, but it is necessary to recognize that a belief in a definite kind of immortality is no longer the force in men's minds that it was two generations ago and that the disappearance of this definiteness and simplicity of religious belief has vastly changed our way of looking at and judging each other. It is not necessary to say that men no longer look forward to a conscious immortality. Many do. But such a faith is not now an instinctive part of our intellectual equipment. The old meaning being gone from life, we must seek a new meaning and a new interpretation, for the assumption of a meaningless life is not to be borne. At this point the new biographer enters.

As yet, the interpretations of life which succeed the older and the orthodox are many and various. To some it is a physical or biological adventure—as to Philip Guedalla. To others a spectacle—as to André Maurois. To some a search—as to Gamaliel Bradford, and in futile, tragic fashion to Henry Adams. And to Lytton Strachey it is a groping for light in a world of shadows viewed by a remote superior being who saw it all with such fitful phosphorescent glow as might be generated by his own inner processes.

And who are the moderns by this test? It is unnecessary to name them all. Nor is this a catalogue of authors. But some must be named. First among the Americans, Gamaliel Bradford, the seeker after souls, the more contradictory the better. It was Bradford who said of himself that he might believe in Heaven if he could imagine a Heaven as interesting as Earth. Then of course Strachey, Maurois, and, for reasons, Philip Guedalla. There are others—many others—but we are seeking for light and understanding and these come better in small groups than in crowds.

Of all the genuine, rather than the accidental, moderns first place must be given to Gamaliel Bradford, the American. It is not that he is greater than Lytton Strachey, although there is a possibility of argument for that conclusion. The fact is that Strachey is only accidentally a biographer at all. His concern with life is that of a philosopher. His viewpoint is that of a despairing perfectionist who would like to find life somewhere complete and beautiful and knows that he never will.

Bradford profits perhaps by being a product of a younger civilization. Crudeness and imperfection are to be expected in the American world and part of the task of the biographer is to find beauty and courage in the clay with which he deals. Perhaps our valiant dust is the more valiant for being dust.

Mr. Bradford's conscious artistry is directed toward the end of revealing and understanding rather than of mocking and despairing. In his introduction to "Wives" he sets up his standards: "The biography must be made interesting, must be made beautiful, must be a well composed, designed, and finished performance."

Here is conscious artistry with a vengeance. Can a life be a well composed, designed, and finished performance? Can a book avoid it— and be worth reading? Of course, the danger of writing a book about anything is that the art necessarily involves plan, unity, climax, and a conclusion. Life itself often merely ends, which is quite different from the dramatic last curtain of the theater or the last chapter of the novel. And yet if biography is to interpret rather than to catalogue and present it must have design, action, and therefore drama.

The best examples of Mr. Bradford's method are to be found in his shorter sketches— "psychographs" he calls them. The facts that appear are few in number and are in the nature of marginal notes, illustrating a point rather than containing it. In "The Quick and the Dead" he says: "It is a marked feature of that method (the psychographic) that it lays stress upon essential elements of character rather than upon the shift and variety of circumstance." The method is an appealing one, but it lays a heavy burden upon the biographer and is dangerous in less than the ablest of hands.

In "The Quick and the Dead" we find him dealing with seven men: Theodore Roosevelt, Wilson, Edison, Ford, Lenin, Mussolini, and Coolidge. What has this queerly assorted company in common except life—and the fact that all but two have been presidents or dictators? Mr. Bradford is prompt with his answer: "Ambition, the intense concern with this world to the exclusion of another, the astonishing readiness to accept responsibility and make critical decisions, the passion for dealing with men and the method of controlling them."

He applies his method even to his titles:

Fury of Living	Roosevelt
Brains Win and Lose	Wilson
Let There Be Light	Edison
Wheel of Fortune	Ford
World as Idea	Lenin
World as Will	Mussolini
Genius of the Average	Coolidge

There is abundant ground for disputing
Mr. Bradford's selections and labels. Why not
Will for Roosevelt or Idea for Wilson? Why
Edison or Coolidge in such a gallery at all?
Evidently there is some doubt in the artist's
mind, as witness this from the sketch of
Coolidge dealing with his Black Hills summer:
"There is the garish cowboy rig, and in the
midst of it the chilly Vermont countenance,
wondering painfully and wearily what it was
all about. These people were not working;
why should anybody want to do anything
but work." And yet the cowboy worked as
hard as any Vermonter and not all Vermonters
worked all the time.

Mr. Bradford has few peers in the art of
summing up a man, however much we may
disagree with some of his generalizations. In
his sketch of Woodrow Wilson he works
toward a conclusion by abundant quotations
from the President's own statements. Then
comes the telling phrase: "He knew, he knew,
he always knew, for he was a creature of
brains." Probably nothing more is needed.
Or consider this on Theodore Roosevelt:
"He killed mosquitoes as if they were lions
and lions as if they were mosquitoes." At least
it catches the imagination.

That is superficial, however, compared with the comment on T. R.'s religion: "I cannot find God insistent or palpable anywhere in the writings or the life of Theodore Roosevelt. He had no need of him and no longing because he really had no need of anything but his own immensely sufficient self." Here is Bradford at his best, brushing aside the ordinary questions of good or bad, right or wrong, moral or immoral, and striking straight at the heart of his subject. Incidentally it is probably the clearest portrait of T. R. ever presented. But what a shock to the orthodox.

Able interpreter as he is, Bradford does not so much explain men as portray them credibly and clearly. The inner mystery of personality remains, but the personality itself leaps out at us, sharp and credible. In fact it is sometimes safe to say that he is most illuminating when he is not too sure. He presents Lenin in his world as Idea, emphasizing his devotion to a cause, referring in a moment of meditation to Lenin's emphasis of his ego and his enjoyment of his power over men. "And then through it all is interwoven that strain of sardonic laughter, which I cannot quite explain or understand. So, as

often with these great doers of the world,
we are forced to end with a question. For
doing, and life, and death, are merely a vast
question after all."

But he is seldom at a loss for the idea neatly
packed in a phrase, almost dazzling in its
directness and completeness. Much has been
written of Lincoln's religion, of proof and
disproof, of guess and hope and criticism.
Bradford sums it up in a sentence: "He
practiced with God the same superb, shrewd
opportunism by which, as contrasted with
the dogmatic idealism of Jefferson Davis,
he saved the American Union."

Of another Lincoln, the wife of the Emanci-
pator, much has been written, mostly con-
jecture when it was not impertinence, and
all of it together not a featherweight in comparison with the opening paragraph in Bradford's chapter on Mrs. Lincoln in "Wives":

"A brilliant but uncouth and almost gro-
tesque lawyer and politician from the backwoods, with no inherited social position or
distinction, marries a showy, popular belle,
who considers herself an aristocrat in the
limited circle which is all she knows, and
feels that she is condescending vastly in
accepting the husband whose only asset is

an extremely nebulous future. Then the husband shows an unexampled capacity for growth and development, intellectual and spiritual, if not social, and the wife, remaining to the end the narrow rural aristocrat she was in the beginning, is decidedly left behind."

This says it all. Nothing more is needed.

Probably the highest point that Bradford reached was in that tragic collection of traitors, fanatics, rebels, and fakers, "Damaged Souls." Look at the list: Benedict Arnold, Thomas Paine, Aaron Burr, John Randolph of Roanoke, John Brown, Phineas Taylor Barnum, and Benjamin Franklin Butler. It is a darkly brilliant, sinister, dangerous company. As Bradford admits, there are wide differences of performance, temperament, and character from Arnold who "sold the personal trust of Washington for a cash reward" to the "noisy, cheap vulgarity of Barnum." And in between are Paine the philosopher of the Revolution, Randolph the mad patriot, and Brown the bloody-handed lover of liberty.

All of them have suffered irreparable damage to their reputations, living and dead, and all of them seem to have suffered "some

inward taint of spiritual obliquity or inadequacy" that groups them together, in
memory, much as they would have disliked
and distrusted each other in life. All were
the slaves of intense, selfish ambition, all
were men of strong passions, although women
and alcohol played small part in their ruin,
all were excessively vain, and all, except perhaps Arnold and Brown, were masters of
words. And they were all terribly concerned
with immediate, practical things.

Bradford does not suggest it, but they were
all men of action of varying kinds for whom
the world as they found it was far too narrow
for their far-leaping desires. Something in
them doomed them to intractability, rebellion,
or treason. Barnum alone was practical enough
to make his unconventionality profitable.
He alone was a good citizen.

The best chapter in the book is that on
Aaron Burr. He is the most charming and
contradictory, and the hardest to describe.
Even Arnold's treason was clear and logical
by contrast. Women loved Burr, too many
and to their own hurt—never to his. "In all
his eighty years he never made the ghastly
discovery that a pretty woman can be a bore."
Men believed in him, even in his wildest

moments. He tied with Jefferson for the
presidency, he shot his archenemy Hamilton,
he was tried for treason and though acquitted
the case against him was black, he wandered
in poverty and exile in Europe, and yet men
could be found to swear by him and children
followed him everywhere. He had wrecked
his own hopes, he had betrayed everyone
who trusted him, except his daughter, he
had gambled carelessly for unpardonably
high stakes, but he was a stranger to remorse.
Late in life he referred casually to "my
friend Hamilton, whom I shot."

What was the inner life of this man who,
as Bradford says, "On that July morning on
the Heights of Weehawken tossed his future
in the air and shot it to pieces like a glass
pigeon, just from a whim of spite, or was it
really from a notion of honor?" Even Bradford can not tell us quite, but he gives us many
glimpses. He was not irreligious—none of
the Damaged Souls were, not even Thomas
Paine whom Theodore Roosevelt called a
dirty little atheist. But was he religious? He
should have been; he was a grandson of
Jonathan Edwards, but his references to
religion are few. Bradford finds that: "In
general, his attitude is that of a polite ac-

quaintance with God, such as he maintained with all gentlemen, but of no particular intimacy. I don't know what can better sum up his religion than his delightful remark: 'I think that God is a great deal better than people suppose.'"

And there is another illustration. "In his last illness a reverend gentleman asked him as to his hope of salvation through Christ. He replied that 'on that subject he was coy.'"

This is the man who in the speech that marked his retirement from the presidency of the Senate said: "On full investigation it will be discovered that there is scarce a departure from order but leads to or is indissolubly connected with a departure from morality."

This is the point at which Bradford ends his chapter on Burr. "It is said that Senators wept. I imagine the angels wept also. Fortunately not even the tears of angels can ever blot out that sentence."

If Bradford had written only "Damaged Souls" he would have earned his crown. But he wrote "American Portraits," "Union Portraits," "Confederate Portraits," "The Quick and the Dead," "Wives," "Robert E. Lee," "D. L. Moody." American literature as well

as American biography is immeasurably the
richer for his work.

I have given first place among the moderns
to Gamaliel Bradford, the American. This is
a rash statement. It is not true in art as it is
in baseball that performances can be scored,
averages compared, the results tabulated,
and the prize awarded. *De gustibus non
disputandum* is still a necessary warning. But
there are tests and canons that lie below
moods and prejudices and tastes. In the
clarity of Bradford's sympathy and tolerance
of his vision and the breadth of his understanding, I am disposed to stand by my
judgment. But yet—

There is Lytton Strachey, an Englishman
by accident of birth, a Frenchman in all those
aspects of mental hardness and detachment,
delicacy of perception and distinction, deft-
ness of expression. He has written three books
which are not likely to be equaled soon. His
"Eminent Victorians," "Queen Victoria,"
and "Elizabeth and Essex" stand by themselves in all the welter of books, good and
bad, that drip from the presses. And yet, as
he is not quite a Frenchman and certainly
not an Englishman, whatever his blood, so

one is not quite sure that he is a biographer. Elsewhere I have referred to his groping for light in a world of shadows. To that should be added that he gropes for light with little hope of finding it. It is as though he had come from another world to view for a little while the curious, futile human struggle, to write down something of what he saw, a trifle condescendingly as is only fair, and then to step back again into the deeper shadow from which he emerged. But he leaves light behind—and envy that we cannot quite understand, much less imitate, his method.

Others have written of Queen Victoria with not always friendly frankness. Many have praised her; a few have condemned. Strachey neither praises nor condemns. Neither is he concerned to magnify the English people. As the grimly ironical, unprejudiced visitor from another world he notes the long panorama of her sixty-four years as queen and empress. This was the woman who sought to dictate the foreign policy of England and took a lively part in the discussion of the kind of beards to be worn by the sailors of the Royal Navy. She demanded war with Russia and saved her childhood dolls and all the souvenirs of her youth. She worshiped her

husband, raged at the faintest trace of dis-
respect to him, retired into almost conventual
seclusion after his death, and so made the
orderly administration of government as difficult as possible, and yet demanded from her
ministers the most complete subjection to
her own will and was vastly indignant when
she did not have it.

The temptation to quote from Strachey is
strong. And yet separate quotations can not
reveal his secret. For secret it is, that method
by which, seeming always to deal with the
most obvious and often trivial material, he
yet produces the effect of the whole. At the
end the woman herself stands out, narrow,
unimaginative, often bad-tempered, arrogant,
rather ignorant although surprisingly liter-
ate, but still for over sixty years Queen,
Empress, Defender of the Faith, and all the
rest. Look at her, a girl of eighteen, at her
first council. "The great assembly of lords
and notables, bishops, generals, and ministers
of state, saw the doors thrown open and a
very short, very slim girl in deep plain mourn-
ing come into the room alone and move forward to her seat with extraordinary dignity
and grace; they saw a countenance, not
beautiful, but prepossessing—fair hair, blue

prominent eyes, a small curved nose, an open
mouth revealing the upper teeth, a tiny chin,
a clear complexion, and, over all, the strangely
mingled signs of innocence, of gravity, of
youth, and of composure."

That was June 20, 1837. There is another
scene, January 22, 1901, the day she died.

"Perhaps her fading mind called up once
more the shadows of the past to float before
it, and retraced, for the last time, the vanished
visions of that long history—passing back and
back, through the cloud of years, to older and
ever older memories—to the spring woods at
Osborne, so full of primroses for Lord Beaconsfield—to Lord Palmerston's queer clothes
and high demeanour, and Albert's face under
the green lamp, and Albert's first stag at
Balmoral, and Albert in his blue and silver
uniform, and the Baron coming in through
a doorway. . . . " So the recital runs on
down to "a yellow rug, and some friendly
flounces of sprigged muslin, and the trees
and the grass at Kensington." And in
between the power and the glory, wealth,
an empire acknowledged, a wonder-century
run through to its warring end. He gives us
Victoria. And does he teach us the importance
of the commonplace? Or is it the triviality

of all things, including the most important?
Could anyone but a visitor from another
world do that?

It is really in some of the shorter works
that one seems to catch a glimpse here and
there of the Strachey method, particularly
in some of the chapters in "Eminent Victorians." Probably it is not so much the method
one sees as Strachey himself, for in the practice
of an art it is an understanding of the artist
that explains.

Probably no one, except perhaps a being
from another world, will ever explain the
tragic Gordon, fanatic, hero, drunkard, mystic,
martyr; but observe Strachey's eye on the
queer influence he seemed to exert on other
supposedly normal beings. "One catches a
vision of strange characters, moved by mysterious impulses, interacting in queer complica-
tion, and hurrying at last—so it almost
seems—like creatures in a puppet show to
a predestined catastrophe."

This is something more than mere biography, though this sentence is perhaps the
philosophy of modern biography. At least
it is Strachey.

It is always the significant absurdities
and contradictions of life that catch him.

Gordon, after being shelved, neglected, forgotten, is chosen as the man to evacuate
Khartoum or to save Egypt; which he was
to do has never been quite clear. He is leaving
Victoria Station on the first stage of his last
journey and half the Cabinet seems there to
bid him Godspeed. Lord Granville buys his
tickets, the Duke of Cambridge opens the
carriage door for him. Lord Wolseley hands
in a bag of gold for the expenses of his journey.
"The train started. As it did so, Gordon
leaned out and addressed a last whispered
question to Lord Wolseley. Yes, it had been
done. Lord Wolseley had seen to it himself;
next morning every member of the cabinet
would receive a copy of Dr. Samuel Clarke's
'Scripture Promises.' That was all. The train
rolled out of the station."

The chapter on Gordon is complete in
its message of tragic futility. Khartoum
fell and his head was set on its shattered
wall. The Mahdi ruled the desert for thirteen years. Then Kitchener came with his
Maxim-Nordenfeldt's, the desert armies were
broken at Omdurman, and memorial services were held in the town that Gordon had
neither evacuated nor held. "It had all
ended very happily—in a glorious slaughter

of 20,000 Arabs, a vast addition to the British Empire, and a step in the peerage for Sir Evelyn Baring." And Baring was the man who least understood and most disliked "Chinese" Gordon.

In all his groping Strachey seeks one thing, the inner core of character—not as good or bad, but as the ultimate reality. He finds much at which to wonder in Florence Nightingale—the Lady with the Lamp. But he finds one trait and makes one profound observation. "Like most great men of action—perhaps like all—she was simply an empiricist. She believed in what she saw, and she acted accordingly; beyond that she would not go."

It is not fair to dismiss Strachey without a word as to his power of presentation. Here was a philosopher—critic—historian—who was also an artist, surely a rare combination. In "Elizabeth and Essex" the narrative moves to the last act in the drama of Philip of Spain. He is dying in his gloomy palace of the Escorial. He alternates between faint touches at the tangled web of diplomacy and frenzied prayers for the repose of his own soul. He recalls the heretics that he has burned and regrets that he had not insured his salvation by burning more. Word comes of a victory of the rebel Tyrone over the English in Ireland and he is cheered. Then he sleeps. "When he awoke, it was night and there was singing at the altar below him; a sacred candle was lighted and put into his hand, the flame, as he clutched it closer and closer, casting lurid shadows upon his face; and so, in ecstasy and in torment, in absurdity and in greatness, happy, miserable, horrible, and holy, King Philip went off to meet the Trinity."

It delights Strachey to prove that life is not lived according to the old copybook maxims. It is easy and comforting to believe that Elizabeth was a great queen because of her wisdom, decisiveness, and courage. Triumph she did, as "Elizabeth and Essex" shows, but "that triumph was not the result of heroism. The very contrary was the case; the grand policy which dominated Elizabeth's life was the most unheroic conceivable; and her true history remains a standing lesson for melodramatists in statecraft. In reality, she succeeded by virtue of all the qualities which every hero should be without—dissimulation, pliability, indecision, procrastination, parsimony."

The facts by which Strachey leads up to and proves this conclusion have been open

to the world for generations. No one else has
made such withering use of them. Evidently
most of us are held too firmly in the grip of
clichés and maxims. Either Strachey's humanity is broader and colder than ours or he
draws from intellectual sources unknown to
the rest of us. Like Henry Adams he stands
alone.

And there is André Maurois, French in
blood and training, an artist with words,
thoroughly at home in every field of literary
criticism, legitimate heir to the best classical
tradition of his nation. He has written lives
of three famous Englishmen, Shelley, Disraeli,
and Byron. He has lectured on biography.
As we have seen, he has a definite concept
of biography as "a story of the evolution
of the human soul." But he is also a novelist,
and fiction and biography are too near akin
to live well together. The marriage of cousins
in a hazardous experiment. Mrs. Gertrude
Atherton proved that with a biographic novel
on Alexander Hamilton, "The Conqueror."

His choice of subject is an indication of the
trend of Maurois's interest: Shelley, the poetic
anarchist among philosophers; Byron, the
rebel poet; Disraeli, the alien peacock among

the sober-plumaged poultry of the English
political barnyard. These betray the strong
romantic leaning of his classical structure.

Of the three, "Disraeli, a Picture of the
Victorian Age," is definitely the best biography. "Ariel," which is the significant title
of his life of Shelley, deals chiefly with the
superficial aspects and adventures of the poet's
life. His political philosophy receives too
scanty presentation and his verse is almost
entirely ignored. And it is Shelley's verse
that gives him warrant for immortality.

When he turned his hand to Byron, Maurois
had learned one lesson, as he admits in the
introduction, and the result is a sound but
uninspired combination of literary history
and criticism. His most individual contribution is in his ascription of certain of the
Byronic verse to particular moods, phases,
and experiences that checkered the poet's
life. Many of the things that made Byron a
sensation and a scandal in London a century
and more ago are dead and should be forgotten. His poems gather dust on library shelves,
and his memory lingers faint and fading, only
an echo of the charm and diablerie that once
made him vivid, fascinating, and notorious.
Probably when Tom Moore yielded to the

urgings of the Gordon family and burned the Byron journal, the chance of a real life of Byron was burned with it.

It is Disraeli that shows us Maurois at his most interesting and most characteristic moment. As we read, though, the suspicion arises that the Disraeli he shows us is Disraeli as a novelist prefers to think he might have been, not Disraeli as a historian found him. Early in the book, on page 19 to be exact, he presents the young prodigy at school!

"With the turmoil of the little schoolboy world, the memories of his intrigues, his triumphs, his miniature wars, had come glimpses, as through scattering clouds, of clear and vivid landscapes; and then he could descry the distant shapes of vast ambition, just as a man drawing near a town will catch sight of the lofty towers soaring above it. Life, it seemed to him, would be intolerable if he were not the greatest among men; not one of the greatest, but quite definitely the greatest."

All this of a restless, precocious boy of fifteen. It is hazardous to read so much into the dreams of adolescence, although much may be permitted to the backward-looking biographer.

Again and again Maurois's romantic vein asserts itself. The young Disraeli has returned from his Grand Tour and flings himself into the dissipated, colorful life of London in the thirties. "London in those days had a Watteau-like charm," the biographer says. He enlarges upon the people and things of the shifting scene, the beautiful Sheridan sisters, Caroline Norton, Wellington, Peel, balls, dinners, evenings at Almack's. Disraeli halts between thoughts of political power and the lure of social success.

"Yes, without a doubt, the game must go on. But sometimes, when some evening party had been charming, when London at night gleamed dimly in the fog as he came out from some ball, when a pretty woman had lingered as she pressed his hand in farewell, he would tell himself that ambition was a vain folly, that this frivolity he had feigned so long was his true nature, and was wisdom too, that it would be delightful to live on forever at the feet of the three Sheridan sisters, a fond and indolent page."

And yet he has assured us previously that Disraeli had gone in for society as the surest road to political success. Is he writing fiction or biography?

At times, however, the reader is tempted to conclude that the romantic view of politics may be the best. Disraeli decides to be a Conservative and Maurois explains his choice.

"For him, to be a Conservative was not just to uphold with an apologetic smile a constitution held to be out of date; it was a proud and romantic attitude, the only intelligent one, the only one which loyally took into account the authentic England, those villages grouped round the manor-house, that vigorous, obstinate breed of small squires, that aristocracy at once so venerable and so assimilative, nay, history itself."

This is picturesque and may be true, except that it does not help us to understand the man who as head of the government administered the most vigorous foreign policy that England was to know for a century. There was such an England as Maurois describes, but his picture fails to remind us that Disraeli was witness to the sunset of aristocracy, and the crowding in of industrialism.

Deathbed scenes are the acid test of the romantic. Guedalla revels in them. Even Strachey is not above using them, as in "Queen Victoria" where he makes the imagined last thoughts of the queen complete his

picture of a long life crowded with statecraft
and war, ministers of state and bishops, dolls,
primroses, days at Balmoral and on the Isle
of Wight, all the lumber and bric-a-brac, big
and little, of the years. Bradford alone seems
able to leave his people to die in decent peace.
Maurois frankly uses what is almost the
dying scene in Disraeli to wring the last
lingering tear from the eye of the reader.

"He went to sit down by the fire in his
library, read a little more, closed his eyes,
and dreamed. The cry of an owl in the old
cypress had evoked Mary Anne's drawn
features, so tired, so dear. He fancied he
could hear the gay chatter which she had
bravely kept up to the very end. A log slipped
down. The old man poked, and there was a
shower of sparks; a brief gleaming of life.
It was nearly fifty years since, in a tiny
drawing-room with white muslin curtains,
he had seen smiling around him those ravish-
ing faces of the Sheridans—Caroline Norton—
how lovely she had been, with her black
tresses and her violet eyes—she had been so
to the end."

This is skillful fiction, but why call it
biography? It is a fair criticism of such
writing to challenge it as an unfair exercise

of the artist's right of deductive creation.
To be sure, Maurois is not often guilty of
such abuse of his power, but it is fair to say
of his Disraeli that he has exaggerated the
superficial at the expense of the inner and the
more important. If Strachey did it we might
conclude that it was because he believed that
there was nothing important there, within
or without. Must we say the same in the case
of Maurois?

When one attempts to place Philip Guedalla
in the gallery of biography the task is not an
easy one. His three portraits, "Palmerston,"
"Wellington," and "The Second Empire"
(Louis Napoleon) are among the most graphic
and dramatic that our time has produced.
It is with the word dramatic that the first
doubt arises. Is it drama or melodrama that
he gives us? That he has a philosophy or a
purpose of biography is clear. He states it
in his "Life of Palmerston":
     "Yet I have always thought that there
is a muse, no less than a method of history;
and using (though, I hope, concealing) the
full apparatus of research and documents,
I have done my best to paint his portrait to catch something of the movement

of his world, and to bring back the dead without sacrifice either of accuracy or of vividness."

Whatever we may think of Guedalla as an exponent of his own philosophy, there can be no doubt that in style and in attitude he is a modern of the moderns. Appraisal there is in plenty, but none of the moral judgments that so often irritated Walter Raleigh, the supercritic. He brings back the dead right enough—Palmerston and Wellington, the eighteenth century survivals, Napoleon the Futile, so that we see them again for a moment, the two brilliant, hard, unflinching, the one dark, furtive, a little wistful; but is it the real men we see or only the shadows they threw on the historical back drop? And when does drama become melodrama?

Let us glance at the evidence. The first and most lasting impression is of a writer intoxicated by his gift of the phrase and his power to make the dead seem to come alive by allusion.

Here is an example from his "Palmerston" to illustrate:

"It was the uneasy, changing world of 1828, which danced on summer nights at

Almack's and observed without undue exhilaration the new palace at Pimlico. The Duke charmed deputations; whilst at the Cottage Majesty indulged a rustic taste, went fishing on Virginia Water, stopped out late and caught royal colds, or crept into London after dark 'when nobody could see his legs or whether he could walk' especially to annoy Mr. Creevey."

Material enough here for an undergraduate examination in English history of the period. Put with it the following from the early days of Louis Napoleon as he appears in the opening chapters of "The Second Empire":

"Then there was an unhappy looking German gentleman, who was the King of Prussia and brought with him to Malmaison two small boys, to one of whom fifty years later Louis was to send his sword on the hill of La Marfee above Sedan."

The latter reads almost like a historical riddle. Who was the small boy and why did Louis send him a sword fifty years later? And why at Sedan?

Mr. Guedalla touches his minor figures deftly and to a vivid end. There is in the "Palmerston" one sentence devoted to "Colonel John Burgoyne of the Light Dragoons,

that intrepid versifier, who set As You Like
It to an air of Mr. Gay and marched through
the dripping woods to Saratoga."

George Bernard Shaw used more than a
full act of "The Devil's Disciple" to paint a
portrait of Burgoyne and did no more than
Guedalla has done in a sentence. It must be
admitted that there is a Guedallan knack
for epigrammatic characterization. There is
the young Francis Joseph at Villa France,
"a tall young man of twenty-eight in a blue
uniform." Could a phrase be more obliterat-
ing? And Frederick the Great, "that tight-
lipped man with hunted eyes." And some
of the entourage at the Tuileries.

"M. de Persigny with his solemn stare,
the wry smile of M. Merimee, Macquard, the
secretary in his buttoned coat . . . and the
suave M. de Morny with his bald head and
his imperial." It's clever, but is it accurate?
Read his line on Louis: "Mostly he was a
kindly, aging man who inflicted parlor games
upon his circle or sat smiling a vague, sleepy
smile through the innumerable scenes of
imperial magnificence."

If that was all, would Louis have been able
to achieve even the empty gesture that was
his? Guedalla is surely happier in his reference

to "the sad, perpetual smile of Eugenie."
At least it is so that she is remembered.

His gift for catching—or at least seeming
to catch—years or volumes in a phrase leads
up many side roads. He pauses a moment in
painting Lord Palmerston to remark: "for
it is the modest aim of English education to
model its pupils on their grandfathers."
Palmerston leads him back to George IV
who finally confers on the English world
the boon of his own death:

"For he had walked his interminable min-
uet, and was beyond them all—beyond the
memory of Fitzherbert and the avenging
furies of Queen Caroline and the tired eyes
of Lady Conyngham."

Sometimes his marginal wanderings are
annoying, particularly when they take a
prophetic tone. Louis and Kinglake in London
contest for the favor of a fair but apparently
slightly frail young lady and Louis wins: "But
Mr. Kinglake bore malice and lived to demonstrate by his subsequent treatment of the
Emperor of the French the unwisdom of
exasperating a historian."

Are we to assume that Kinglake wrote his
laborious "Invasion of the Crimea" to get
square with his successful rival of thirty years

earlier? Often the phrases are smart for no
other apparent reason than to be smart.
"There was an agreeable spontaneity about
the Revolution of 1848 which it shares with
the best earthquakes."

It is possible to understand this, although
it indicates a rather casual survey of the
events leading up to 1848, but what, if anything, does Mr. Guedalla mean when he
says, also in "The Second Empire," "The
Caucasian races have always preferred their
heroes slightly bronzed."

It is in his death scenes that Guedalla
gives himself away as the sentimentalist
that he is. For reasons which do not now
matter, Hortense, the daughter of Josephine,
had sung an old song to her mother and
to Napoleon before the battle of Wagram,
" . . . and twenty-five years later, when
the Emperor and his Empress were both dead
four thousand miles apart, Hortense sang
the old song in exile for Dumas." What of
it?

Occasionally, but only occasionally, his
words are too much for him. That happens,
for example, when he takes a look at the future
of Francis Joseph: "But half a century away
he was to fade dismally out of life in the

thunder of a twilight of half the gods in Europe
. . . . " Is this fine writing or just bad English?
The two are not always easily distinguishable.

Usually his ironic instinct and his crafts-
manship save him by at least a hair. Two
cases where he walks close to the edge of the
pit of bathos are in the closing scenes of Louis
Napoleon at Chislehurst and of the young
Prince Victor in the Zulu War in South
Africa. Of Napoleon he says, "As he drowsed
into the last unconsciousness he muttered
something to Conneau about Sedan; those
thudding guns under that leaden sky haunted
him to the end, and the story was over."

The death of the Prince Imperial is the
carefully calculated closing scene of an era as
well as of a biography:

"Then as the galloping horses pounded
away into the distance he walked slowly
toward the Zulus with a revolver in his left
hand. Three shots were fired, before the long
spears flashed; and they left him stripped in
the trampled grass."

Then comes the familiar allusiveness, smack-
ing of the historical riddle—"The sun which
had set over Longwood and Schönbrunn and
Chislehurst went down behind Itelezi. Only
the Empress lived on."

Is it good biography or high class melodrama? The present witness refuses to commit
himself, further than to warn aspiring young
biographers that, as is so often the case, the
cleverest of craftsmen is sometimes the most
dangerous of models. It is safer to admire
Mr. Guedalla than to imitate him.

XVII

THE LAST WORD

No ONE is more aware than the author of the inadequacy of this brief flight over the field of English biography. The subject is too large and too varied for more than a glimpse here and there. There are so many names, large and small—and not always are the large ones the more important. To attempt to name and describe them all would be to produce merely an annotated catalogue. For that reason it has been necessary to choose and to reject. With the choices there is abundant room to quarrel. My reasons for a choice have always been clear and satisfactory to myself. Some have been historical, a few literary, all of them have seemed to carry us forward a step or to illuminate a turn in the corridor of time. Others might have been chosen here and there but they were not.

It has been difficult to find a satisfactory ending, for life does not end. It merely changes a little and goes on. That is a biological and not a theological statement. But an arbitrary stopping point must be made. Hence the chapter on The Moderns.

I must confess to more dissatisfaction with this than with any other part of the book. Why choose only four? Partly because they are important, interesting, and different. Partly because they are characteristically modern. Partly because they are all generally alike in the essential aspects of their modernity. And partly because—well, partly because it pleased me to do it.

I do not entirely like the more critical mood in which this chapter was written. It is a little out of the vein of the rest of the book. But it seems to me that the moderns are fairer game for criticism than are the others. They are of our time and, if we can not deal a trifle harshly with our own, with whom can we? They are playing a considerable part in shaping the thinking and writing of our time and so must be chastised for the good of our own souls, if not of theirs.

I regret the many omissions from this chapter. Why have I not given space to Emil Ludwig? Frankly because, with the possible exception of his "Napoleon," his work does not seem to me important. It is high-grade journalism, but not marked with either the results of special research or an especially high order of creative thinking. I should apologize to Lloyd Lewis for not mentioning his "Sherman—Fighting Prophet." If he had written another book as good as this admirable volume it could not have been denied a place. Captain Liddell-Hart is a rare combination—a military man who can write and who knows the art of war and at the same time does not appear to regard war as the supreme end of existence. Captain Thomason of the Marines has dealt effectively with "Beauty" Stuart of the Confederate cavalry. If he can subdue a little the fervor of this book, without losing his fine enthusiasm, there is a long list of Civil War commanders who will be the better for some attention from Captain Thomason.

Francis Hackett has given us an exciting "Life of Henry VIII," and anyone who can make that redoubtable Tudor exciting, after his long sleep, has done something worth while. Mr. Hackett has a real literary gift for biography, discriminating, sympathetic, and controlled. His book is much better than the brief space I give it would indicate. Perhaps a taste will indicate its quality. Henry VII has died and been buried in St. Paul's and London

222   THE GREAT BIOGRAPHERS

streets have cleared. "A fresh air came from
the meadows of Finsbury. The evening light, a
dim blue crystal, bathed once again the
deserted houses. Blue shadows washed the
black-beamed walls. A star rose over a thatched
roof. At St. Paul's they would be praying.
Tomorrow at Westminster the great officers
of state would break their white wands and
cast them into Henry's grave. . . . And when
all of the kings were buried, the month of May
would still come of an evening and whisper
eternity in a London street." Compare this
with one of Guedalla's deathbed scenes.

I want to make it quite clear that I am not
omitting any of the moderns through malice
or ignorance. Thomas Beer has done more than
justice to Mark Hanna and to Stephen Crane
—an odd pair to be sure—but both books are
in the nature of literary *tours de force*. Pringle's
"Theodore Roosevelt" and Allan Nevins's
"Grover Cleveland" are solid and reliable.
There will be few if any better lives of Franklin
than the partially Americanized Frenchman
Fay has written. Chinard's "Thomas Jefferson" is good—if not distinguished. So is
Tyler Dennett's "John Hay," except that the
diplomatic chapters are rather dull. But then
diplomacy is usually rather dull.

So the list runs. There are others who deserve a place, but one must make an ending. Biography has arrived. It competes with fiction for position on the list of best sellers. It is recognized by historians as a genuine contribution in their field and by literary artists as an authentic form of creation. Readers welcome new titles as an addition to their intellectual entertainment. Courses in biography are being offered in college, but whether as English or history—or both—or neither—is yet uncertain. Probably it will develop as a mixture of both—and as something more. Perhaps we are learning at last that the proper study of mankind is man.